Breakaway

Student's Book Four

David Bolton and Lennart Peterson

Nelson

Contents

EXPONENTS	RECYCLING
Martin never helps. *How often do you use a computer? I often do.* *Shall we go somewhere?* *What shall we do? I don't care.* *They were walking on the beach when they found a bottle.*	present simple, including the *do*-construction third person singular *-s* adverbs of frequency past simple past continuous
Don't be late home! *You don't know how lucky you are!* *When are you going to tidy your room?* *I'm receiving you.* *We're landing in two minutes.* *Well done!* *She was pleased with herself.*	past simple, including the *do*-construction *going to* future present continuous past simple reflexive pronouns
Girls are taller than boys. *They grow more slowly.* *He is the tallest.* *We're going to the cinema tonight.* *I'm sorry. What was that?* *It has to be done.* *I don't have to go to school.* *There's no need to think about it.* *Don't write on walls.*	comparatives and superlatives present continuous verb + gerund imperatives
It's big enough. *There aren't enough bedrooms.* *It's not too big.* *May we come in?* *However quiet you are a rattlesnake will hear you.*	various question forms *can, may, could*
She may have gone home. *She must have missed the bus.* *I shouldn't say this.* *You ought to phone her.* *It's rather heavy.*	present simple modal verbs past simple
He could track animals. *He's walking more slowly.* *He knows we're following him.* *It was a 1.3-metre porpoise.*	*can/can't* present continuous present perfect simple

	STRUCTURES	FUNCTIONS
Unit seven page 49	*something, somebody, someone, nobody, no one, anybody, anything, everybody* *so/because* verb + gerund	giving reasons describing results expressing dislike
Unit eight page 57	verb + participle verb + object + participle *everything, everywhere, everybody, everyone every/each*	describing past events talking about numbers and statistics
Unit nine page 65	the article and zero article *much/many, a lot of/plenty of, several, the most, the least*	talking about relations and families talking about numbers and quantities
Unit ten page 73	word formation *while/during* *able to/unable to* past simple passive	talking about numbers and units of measurement talking about ability
Unit eleven page 81	superlatives passives – present simple, present continuous, present perfect uses of *have*	describing people asking for information
Unit twelve page 89	prepositons of place and movement	describing movement and location describing a sequence of events
Unit thirteen page 97	*will* (future) *may, might* gerund constructions past perfect	talking about future probabilities expressing disbelief talking about fulfilled/unfulfilled expectations
Unit fourteen page 105	*must* *so* + adjective adverbs of manner	comparing things talking about obligation and necessity
Unit fifteen page 113	revision – see RECYCLING	telling a narrative giving reasons

EXPONENTS		RECYCLING
It looks something like a sausage. *Somebody forgot to give them back.* *It tasted revolting so nobody bought it.*	*They start making remarks.* *I hate being different.*	partitive nouns present simple *Why . . . ? Because . . .*
He lay sleeping. *He heard a voice talking.* *They spread everywhere.*		past simple numbers and statistics
He visited laboratories at the university. *He's in hospital.*	*Eat plenty of vitamins.* *Blondes have the most hair.*	past perfect countable and uncountable nouns
While the sun was shining we were all right. *He was unable to understand why.* *They were sent two tickets to a play.*		past continuous
They are the most popular teenagers. *Half of them are sent to summer camps.* *They are being given a pep talk.*	*I haven't been offered money yet.* *He let me have a go.*	past simple passive
They take trips around Liberty Island. *Later the same day it came to the surface.*		past simple passive questions
They will probably be powered by electricity. *Trains may use magnetic levitation.* *It's no use telling them.* *You're not serious!*	*He'd learnt very little English.* *He was relieved.*	comparisons interrogative pronouns past simple
It's not so easy. *It's so bad you wouldn't drink it if it was free!*		*must/mustn't* comparatives *have to*
He was waiting at the front door. *He made too much noise so he woke the baby.* *He was caught the next day.*		*wh* – questions past continuous *so/because* past simple passive

1

STEP ONE *Back home*

Every day after school it's always the same – well, more or less the same. Off the bus, up the hill, round the corner, through the gate. Panic! Where's my front door key? A desperate search. Then I find it. I unlock the door. Fantastic – I have the whole house to myself!

I go up to my room and get out my drums. For half an hour I can practise and there's nobody around to complain about the noise. I often imagine myself as the drummer in a rock band. Martin, my older brother, says I haven't got a chance. He's like that, my brother – always cheerful and optimistic!

Then *he* comes home – Martin, I mean. He's eighteen. (I'm sixteen.) He's in his last year at school. He's taking exams at the moment, so we're all treating him with care. The sooner he leaves school, the better, I reckon. He usually comes into my room and starts using my computer. He doesn't even ask me first! It's only a basic model. It hasn't got much memory. But he hasn't got a computer at all. He spends all his money on taking girls out.

Then dad comes home, tired as usual, and sits down in front of the news on television. My mother, who also goes out to work and is just as tired, rushes around and gets supper ready for the whole family. Martin never helps – 'I'm revising!' he shouts down. I sometimes lay the table, at least.

And then we all sit down and eat. And that's how it is, every day.

Daniel Stevens, 5B

1. Ask Daniel Stevens

Work in pairs. One of you is Daniel.

Example: Ask Daniel how old he is. *How old are you?*
I'm sixteen.

Now ask Daniel

1 where he practises on his drums.
2 how long he practises for.
3 how old his brother is.
4 why they are treating Martin with care.
5 if he has a computer.
6 if it has much memory.
7 why his brother hasn't got a computer.
8 if his parents go out to work.
9 if his father helps to get supper ready.
10 what he does instead.

2. The same or different?

Write sentences about Daniel Stevens and compare yourself with him.

Examples: *Daniel is sixteen, and so am I.*
Daniel is sixteen, but I'm fifteen.

1 Daniel/5B
2 He/the drums
3 He/himself/drummer/rock band
4 He/brother/eighteen
5 He/computer
6 His father/the news/television
7 His mother/out/work
8 He/the table/supper

Compare your answers in class.

3. Find out

Ask a friend how often he/she does various things.

Example: *How often do you lay the table?*
I often do.

Use one of these words in your answers:

always usually often sometimes never

Ask how often he/she

1 panics because he/she can't find his/her key.
2 practises on a musical instrument.
3 imagines himself/herself in a rock band.
4 uses a computer.
5 spends money on taking someone out.
6 watches the news on television.
7 gets supper ready for his/her family.
8 lays the table.

4. What about you?

Describe in a few lines what *you* usually do after school.

STEP TWO Indecision

Him: Hello.
Her: Hi.
Him: How are things?
Her: All right, I suppose.
Him: Are you doing anything special?
Her: No, not really.
Him: Well, shall we go somewhere?
Her: I don't mind.
Him: Well, would you like to?
Her: It depends.
Him: How do you mean?
Her: It depends on where *you* want to go.
Him: Well, where do *you* want to go?
Her: I don't care.
Him: Well, I don't mind either. Anywhere *you* like.
Her: No, you say.
Him: Well, why don't we just go for a walk?
Her: A *walk*? There's no point in just walking.
Him: No, I suppose not. Shall we just stay here, then?
Her: No, there's no point in going nowhere.
Him: What shall we do, then?
Her: I don't mind.

5. A dialogue

Complete this dialogue and then practise it with a friend.

– Hello.
– ______ .
– How ______ things?
– ______ right, ______ suppose.
– ______ we ______ for a walk?
– I ______ mind.

6. Mini dialogues

Practise these four dialogues in pairs. You can also think of your own answers.

– How are things?
– *All right, I suppose.*

– Shall we go somewhere?
– *I don't mind.*

Now change the words in italics to:

1 OK, thanks.
2 Not too bad, I suppose.
3 All right, thanks.

1 It depends.
2 Yes, if you like.
3 Yes, OK.

– Where do you want to go?
– *I don't care.*

– Shall we go for a walk?
– *There's no point in just walking.*

Now change the words in italics to:

1 It depends.
2 I don't mind.
3 Anywhere you like.

1 No, I don't want to.
2 Yes, why not?
3 Yes, good idea.

7. Make suggestions

Make suggestions using this table. Practise in pairs.

Shall we Why don't we Would you like to	go somewhere? go for a walk? sit down? go out? just talk? just stay here?	It depends. I don't mind. I don't care.

8. What do you think?

Which of the following do you think is true?

1 She wants him to go away.
2 She doesn't want to go anywhere, but she wants him to stay.
3 She wants to go somewhere, but not with him.
4 He's more interested in her than she is in him.
5 She's interested in him but she doesn't want him to know.

Now discuss your answers in class.

STEP THREE — *The mystery of the Southern Star*

One day in 1898, a fisherman, Matthew Franklin, was repairing his boat on the beach near Portland, Maine, when he suddenly saw a large sailing ship less than a kilometre away. It was sailing straight towards the beach. It was coming closer and closer. It would run aground if it didn't turn soon!

Franklin ran to the water's edge and shouted a warning. But it was too late. The ship was heading in his direction, still under full sail. It ran aground about two hundred metres from the beach. Franklin quickly rowed out to the ship, which was called the *Southern Star*. There was no one on deck, so he shouted, 'Is there anybody there?' There was no reply.

Franklin climbed on board. No sailors were waiting to meet him. He went below deck. Coffee was boiling on the stove, and there were five plates of half-eaten food on the table. Everything was in place. There was no sign of violence. Franklin looked around but there was no crew anywhere on board. The ship was completely deserted. He was just leaving when he noticed a dog in a dark corner. It was shivering. The dog knew the answer to the mystery, but it couldn't tell anybody what it was.

A few weeks later, two boys were walking on a beach near Norfolk, Virginia, when they found a bottle. In it was a note which said, 'Only five of my crew are left. Twenty-eight have disappeared. What's happening?' The page was torn from the log of the *Southern Star*!

9. Ask and answer

Complete the questions and then answer them in pairs.

1 What ______ Matthew Franklin doing when he first saw the *Southern Star*?
2 In which direction ______ it heading?
3 ______ it sailing under full sail?
4 ______ any sailors waiting to meet him on board?
5 Where ______ the coffee boiling?
6 Where ______ the dog hiding?
7 What ______ it doing?
8 Where ______ the two boys walking?

10. Why?

Complete these sentences with your own ideas.

1 The ship ran aground because . . .
2 No sailors were waiting to meet him because . . .
3 Coffee was still boiling on the stove because . . .
4 There was no sign of violence because . . .
5 The dog was shivering because . . .
6 The crew of the *Southern Star* disappeared because . . .

Compare your ideas with other students'.

11. Matthew Franklin's diary

Matthew Franklin kept a diary. In it he wrote down what happened that day in 1898. Complete this page from his diary in your own words.

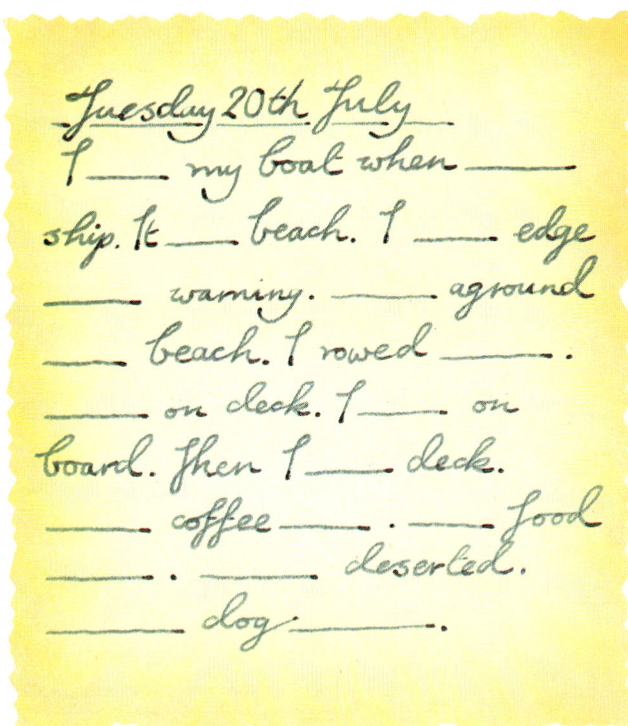
Tuesday 20th July
I ___ my boat when ___
ship. It ___ beach. I ___ edge
___ warning. ___ aground
___ beach. I rowed ___.
___ on deck. I ___ on
board. Then I ___ deck.
___ coffee ___. ___ food
___. ___ deserted.
___ dog ___.

12. Listening

Mark the word you hear.

1	day / die				
2	who / how	5	first / fast	8	tired / tied
3	walk / work	6	money / many	9	least / list
4	mean / men	7	boat / boot	10	ran / run

STEP FOUR ***Applying for a visa***

This form is produced by the Australian immigration authorities. Before you study it, look at these questions.

1 When would you fill in this form? (a) before buying your tickets (b) after buying your tickets but before departure (c) on arrival in Australia

2 Who would not *have to fill in this form?*

Now look through the application form. By the end of it you should be able to discuss your answers to the questions above.

Application to visit Australia – (Please Complete in BLOCK Letters)

IT IS ESSENTIAL THAT VALID PASSPORT/S ACCOMPANY THIS APPLICATION – SEE NOTE (c)

1. FAMILY NAME

2. GIVEN NAMES

3. NAME IN ETHNIC SCRIPT (if applicable)

4. PREVIOUS NAMES

4a. Were your parent(s) or grand parent(s) born in Australia ☐ Yes ☐ No

5. PARTICULARS OF BIRTH Date ..../............../.............. Day Month Year — Town/Village — Country

6. SEX ☐ Male ☐ Female

7. MARITAL STATUS ☐ Married ☐ Never Married ☐ Widowed ☐ Separated ☐ Divorced

8. OCCUPATION

9. PRESENT CITIZENSHIP

10. FULL POSTAL ADDRESS IN UNITED KINGDOM

.... Number and Street .... Suburb or Village

.... City or County .... Post Code

.... Telephone Number

11. PASSPORT DETAILS Number — Place of issue — Date of issue ..../............/............ Day Month Year — Valid until ..../............/............ Day Month Year

12. PURPOSE OF INTENDED VISIT TO AUSTRALIA

Holiday ☐ Business ☐ Visit Relatives ☐ Medical Treatment ☐

13. CONTACT ADDRESS IN AUSTRALIA (if visiting relatives state name and relationship. If visiting for business state name of business contacts, and if visiting for medical treatment state name of doctor/hospital).

14. LENGTH OF STAY (in days or months)

15. PROPOSED DATE OF: (A) Departure from UK ..../............../..............
(B) Arrival in Australia ..../............../.............. Day Month Year

16 (a) DETAILS OF PREVIOUS VISITS TO AUSTRALIA

16 (b) DETAILS OF PREVIOUS APPLICATIONS TO ENTER AUSTRALIA FOR ANY PURPOSE (including migration)

17. PARTICULARS OF FAMILY MEMBERS ACCOMPANYING (see item 'b' of attached visitor visa information)

Full Name	Relationship to Applicant	Date of Birth	Sex

TRAVEL TICKETS SHOULD NOT BE PAID FOR BEFORE A VISA IS OBTAINED

13. Reading comprehension

The following statements contain answers to questions on the application form. Which questions do they answer?

Example: 'My first name's Helen and my middle name's Anne.'
Question 2 ('given names')

1 'It's 051 2468071.'
2 'I'm a student.'
3 'For three weeks.'
4 'To stay with an aunt.'
5 'I'm British.'
6 'I'm leaving on 21 June.'
7 'I live at 68, Granby Road, Edge Hill, Liverpool.'
8 'I'm single.'
9 'c/o Nayre, 15, Coongoola Street, Dandenong, Melbourne, Victoria.'
10 'This is my first visit.'

14. Listening comprehension

Fill in the Australian visa form with the information you hear on the tape.

15. Writing

Fill in a similar application form with information about yourself. Give imaginary answers where necessary.

16. Discussion

1 Do you think you will ever emigrate? Which country would you choose?
2 'People who want to emigrate should be made to pay back the cost of their education.' Do you agree?

Grammar summary

I You We They	come	home.
He She It	comes	

Do	I you we they	help?
Does	he she it	

I You We They	do	(n't).
He She It	does	

It is	always usually often sometimes never	the same.

I He She It	was	walking on the beach when	I he she it we you they	saw something.
We You They	were			

He	always usually often sometimes never	helps.

STEP ONE *How typical are your parents?*

How well do you get on with your parents? Even if the answer's 'very well', there are probably times when you just wish they wouldn't keep on at you. It seems parents the world over have a habit of using a number of well-worn phrases when they're talking to their teenage sons and daughters.

An English magazine for teenagers recently included the following questionnaire to help its readers find out how typical *their* parents were.

How often do your parents say to you . . .

	always	often	some-times	never
1 Don't be late home!	☐	☐	☐	☐
2 If you don't do your homework, you'll never pass any exams.	☐	☐	☐	☐
3 You don't call that awful noise *music*, do you?	☐	☐	☐	☐
4 No, you can't! You're too young.	☐	☐	☐	☐
5 Why don't you listen when I'm talking to you?	☐	☐	☐	☐
6 You don't know how lucky you are. When *I* was your age . . .	☐	☐	☐	☐
7 You don't care how much things cost nowadays . . .	☐	☐	☐	☐
8 My parents didn't let me do that when I was your age.	☐	☐	☐	☐
9 When are you going to tidy your room? It looks as if a bomb's dropped in there!	☐	☐	☐	☐
10 You can't have *everything* you want!	☐	☐	☐	☐
11 How much longer are you going to look at yourself in that mirror?	☐	☐	☐	☐
12 We only want what's best for you.	☐	☐	☐	☐
13 You're not going to go out looking like *that*, are you?	☐	☐	☐	☐

1. What's missing?

Put

do	don't	does	doesn't	did	didn't

into the following sentences.

1 I ______ ______ my homework last night.
2 ______ forget your homework!
3 You ______ call this early, ______ you?
4 My parents ______ let me ______ that when I was your age.
5 You can't go out if you ______ ______ your homework.
6 You ______ tidy your room this morning, ______ you?
7 Parents ______ always know what's best for you, ______ they?
8 My father ______ like the music I play but my mother ______ .

2. Write the dialogue

Parent	**Son or daughter**
Ask if he/she knows how late it is.	Say you don't.
Tell him/her the time.	Express surprise.
Ask where he/she has been.	Answer.
Ask why he/she is so late.	Answer.

Now practise the dialogue you have written in pairs. Change roles.

3. A survey

Ask the other students in the class the questions in the questionnaire. To find out who has the most typical parents, give three points for 'always', two points for 'often', one point for 'sometimes' and no points for 'never'. The parents with the highest total are the most typical!

STEP TWO Contact

As soon as Steven Hamilton had finished his supper it was always the same. 'I'm just going outside for a few minutes', he said to the rest of his family. 'Outside' meant his shed at the bottom of the garden where he had his shortwave radio.

One summer evening he was turning the knobs of his radio set and listening to voices from all over the world. Suddenly he heard a strange, high-pitched voice. It was very weak, but he could just hear the words, repeated over and over again, 'Is there anybody down there? Is there anybody down there?' Steven quickly grabbed his transmitter. 'Yes, this is 3429ZX. I'm receiving you!'

The strange voice came back. 'We are from another galaxy – hundreds of light years from your planet. We are exploring your galaxy, looking for signs of life.'

Steven couldn't believe it. Was *he* going to be the first person on earth to make contact with, and meet, visitors from outer space?

'We're coming down to investigate', said the weird voice. 'We've located the exact position of your radio transmitter. We're landing in two minutes precisely.' 'But there's no room to land here. . .!' There was no reply.

Steven went to the window and looked out. The sky was empty. 'I can't see you!' he shouted into the transmitter. 'We're landing in ten seconds in front of your station. 10 . . . 9 . . . 8 . . . 7 . . . 6 . . . 5 . . . 4 . . . 3 . . . 2 . . . 1 . . . We've landed!' Steven ran out of the shed and looked all round the small back garden. He could see nothing.

He turned to go back into his shed, bitterly disappointed. It was then that he heard a crunching sound. He looked down. Under his right foot a small saucer-shaped object lay broken into a thousand pieces.

4. Interview Steven Hamilton

Complete these questions and then answer them. Work in pairs.

1 Where ______ you keep your shortwave radio?
2 ______ you spend much time there?
3 When ______ you hear this strange voice?
4 ______ it very loud?
5 How ______ you feel?
6 Why ______ they want to land?
7 ______ there enough room to land?
8 ______ you see anything outside?
9 What ______ you do when you went outside?
10 How ______ you feel now?

5. What about the verbs?

Tell the story in the present. Use the present simple or the present continuous forms of the verbs in brackets.

Steve Hamilton ([1] spend) a lot of time in his shed. He often ([2] say): 'I ([3] go) outside for a few minutes.' He ([4] talk) to strangers all over the world. When he ([5] hear) a strange voice he ([6] grab) his transmitter. 'I ([7] receive) you,' he ([8] say). 'We ([9] explore) your universe. We ([10] come) down to investigate your planet. We ([11] know) your exact position. We ([12] land) in two minutes.' When Steven ([13] run) out of his shed, he (not [14] see) the small object which ([15] lie) on the ground.

6. A commentary

At the same time as they are talking to Steven, the visitors from outer space are telling their base back home what they are doing.

Write the commentary starting from the moment they make contact with Steven to when he steps on them. Start like this:

'We are exploring a galaxy hundreds of light years away . . .'

7. Listening

Listen to the voices on the tape and fill in the boxes below.

	Call sign	Country	Local time
Voice 1			
Voice 2			
Voice 3			

STEP THREE *The result*

I wanted to run but I forced myself to walk slowly. When I got to school, I told myself, over and over again, 'Keep calm!'

Suddenly, three boys burst out of the main doors. They couldn't keep it to themselves any longer. 'They've come! They've come!' they yelled. 'What are they like?' I asked one of them. 'You've passed,' he said. I stared at him for a moment. 'I don't believe you,' I said. 'Go and see for yourself, then,' he said. Could I trust him? No, I had to see for myself.

I walked round the corner, but when I was out of sight I ran up the steps, three at a time. The results were on the notice board in our classroom. The girl who sat in front of me was there. She was obviously pleased with herself. 'Well done, Sophie,' she said. So it was true!

My three best friends had passed too. For some reason we laughed and laughed – with relief, I suppose. We just couldn't control ourselves.

But not everyone passed, of course. The ones who knew they were going to fail had prepared themselves. They just said, 'So what?' But then there were the in-betweens, the ones who might have passed but didn't. The boy who sat behind me in class was one of these. He was standing by himself, looking out of the window, furiously angry. He didn't know what to say. Neither did I.

'You're all very pleased with yourselves, I see. But I didn't really expect to pass,' he went on, bitterly. But I knew that wasn't true, and he knew it, too. Then, with his head down, he just slouched out of the room. Even his back looked defeated. All my feeling of joy went with him.

8. Interview Sophie

Complete the questions and answer them. Work in pairs.

1 ______ you pass the exam?
2 ______ you believe the boy who first told you?
3 Where ______ the results?
4 ______ your friends pass?
5 ______ everybody in the class pass?
6 What ______ the ones who failed say?
7 Why ______ one boy very angry?
8 Why ______ you feel happy after that?
9 How ______ you feel now?

9. Make true sentences

You all look very pleased with	myself	if you don't believe me.
She forced	yourself	when we saw the results.
The boy was standing by	himself	because they knew they'd fail.
Go and see for	herself	to walk slowly.
I wanted to see for	ourselves	near the window.
We couldn't control	yourselves	he said.
They had prepared	themselves	if I had passed.

10. Congratulations

Practise congratulating people using:

Well done!
Congratulations!
Fantastic!

Work in pairs and respond to the following:

1 I've passed the exam.
2 I've finished my homework.
3 I got the job.
4 We won the match.
5 I broke the record.

Now think of your own examples.

11. I failed!

Rewrite the story, but this time imagine that Sophie *failed* the exam.

STEP FOUR **Bear care**

This sign can be seen in the Yosemite National Park, California. Before you read it, look at these questions.
1 Why do bears come to camping sites in the park?
2 What do they do there?
3 Why is this not good for them?
4 How can you stop bears taking your food?
Now read the notice. By the end of it you should know the answers to the four questions above. Answer them orally.

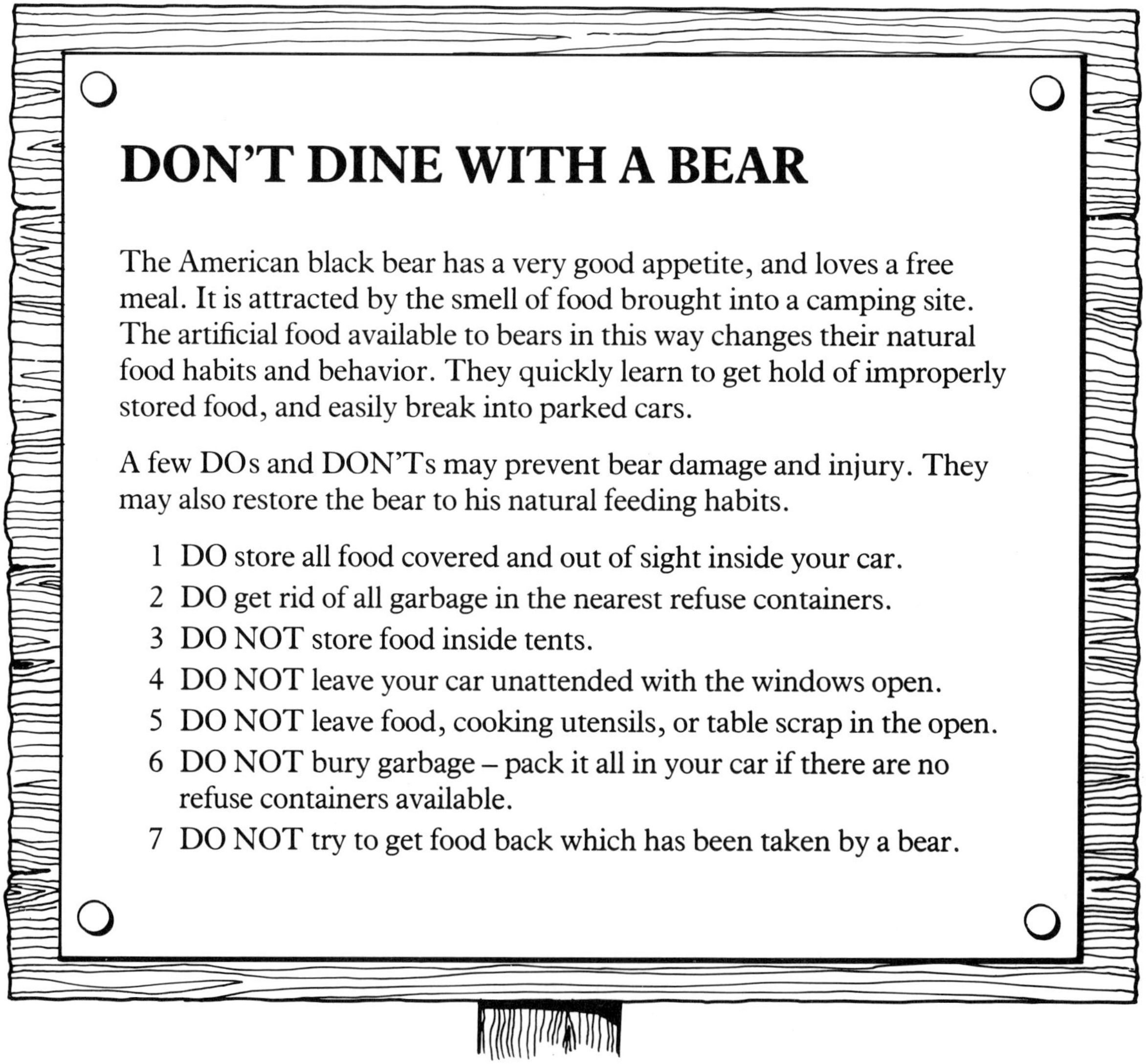

DON'T DINE WITH A BEAR

The American black bear has a very good appetite, and loves a free meal. It is attracted by the smell of food brought into a camping site. The artificial food available to bears in this way changes their natural food habits and behavior. They quickly learn to get hold of improperly stored food, and easily break into parked cars.

A few DOs and DON'Ts may prevent bear damage and injury. They may also restore the bear to his natural feeding habits.

1 DO store all food covered and out of sight inside your car.
2 DO get rid of all garbage in the nearest refuse containers.
3 DO NOT store food inside tents.
4 DO NOT leave your car unattended with the windows open.
5 DO NOT leave food, cooking utensils, or table scrap in the open.
6 DO NOT bury garbage – pack it all in your car if there are no refuse containers available.
7 DO NOT try to get food back which has been taken by a bear.

Now read the notice again. If possible, work out the meaning of new words or, if you can't, look them up in a dictionary.

12. Reading comprehension

Are the following statements true or false?

1 People are allowed to camp in the Yosemite National Park.
2 People bring food to the park to feed the bears.
3 Bears only come to the camp sites because there is not enough natural food available in the park.
4 Bears cannot break into the refuse containers in the park.
5 Bears sometimes break into tents.
6 People eat in the open on the camp sites.

13. Listening comprehension

Listen to the voices on the tape and write down the number of the 'rule' they are breaking.

14. Writing

Write a sign which you might expect to see in a National Park in your country. In it you should describe a particular wild animal found in that park. Then list a few DOS and DON'TS for visitors to the park.

15. Discussion

1 Are any wild animals in your country in danger? What should be done to help them?
2 'Animals have no feelings.' Do you think this is true?

Grammar summary

Don't	be late home!

I You We They	don't	care.
He She It	doesn't	

I You He She It We You They	wanted to see for	myself. yourself. himself. herself. itself. ourselves. yourselves. themselves.

Did	I you he she we you they	do the homework?

Yes, (No,)	I you he she we you they	did	(n't).

I	am	exploring this galaxy. landing in two minutes.
You	are	
He She It	is	
We You They	are	

I	am	going to	go out.
You	are		
He She It	is		
We You They	are		

STEP ONE *You've grown!*

The following graph shows how fast the average American boy or girl grows.

For the first ten years, girls and boys grow at almost exactly the same speed. Then girls suddenly start to grow more quickly than boys. As a result, girls at the age of 13 are taller, heavier and stronger than boys.

At about the age of 14, the average girl starts to grow less rapidly and the average boy catches up and then passes her. Unlike girls, boys do not stop growing when they are 15 or 16. They go on growing, although more and more slowly, until they are about 20. Then they begin to shrink, very slowly but surely. Their weight, however, usually goes on increasing until they are in their 40s.

During adolescence, your face, and particularly the lower half, suddenly changes its shape. Your jaw becomes longer and sticks out more. As a result, your chin becomes much more pointed and your mouth becomes wider. At the same time your nose also becomes slightly longer. In other words, you lose your 'baby-face'.

1. Comparisons

Compare boys and girls in any way you like, using the graph.

1 at the age of 10
2 how fast they grow between 10 and 12
3 their height at the age of 13
4 their weight at the age of 13
5 how fast they grow between 14 and 16
6 their height at the age of 16
7 how much they grow between the ages of 16 and 20
8 their weight at the age of 18

2. Comparing faces

Compare these two faces using these adjectives.

(hair) – long/short
(ears) – pointed/round
(nose) – large/small
(chin) – pointed/round
(mouth) – wide/small
(eyes) – large/small

3. A survey

Find out the average age, height and weight of the students in your class. If there are boys *and* girls, separate them and then compare them.

How do they compare with the statistics for the average American boy/girl?

Who is the youngest/oldest/tallest/shortest/lightest/heaviest student in the class?

STEP TWO *The same but different*

'American English and British English. They're more or less the same, aren't they? Only the accent is different.'

True or not? Read this and then decide for yourself.

I'm dating a cute girl tonight. We're going to a movie downtown.

I'm going out with a nice girl tonight and we're going to the cinema in the town centre.

We're going on vacation to Florida next fall. But gas is getting so expensive that we're going by railroad.

We're having a holiday in Florida next autumn. But petrol is so expensive that we're going by railway.

I left my apartment, took the elevator down to the first floor, walked along the sidewalk, over the crosswalk and then went into a pharmacy.

I left my flat, took the lift down to the ground floor, walked along the pavement, over the pedestrian crossing and then went into a chemist's.

I want some cookies, candies and a bag of potato chips.

I'd like some biscuits, some sweets and a packet of crisps, please.

4. Dialogues

Write short dialogues in which the British person asks the American to repeat what he said.

Example: **American:** I'm going on vacation to California next fall.
Englishman: *I'm sorry, what was that?*
American: *I mean I'm going on holiday to California next autumn.*

1 I'm buying an apartment downtown next month.
2 I just bought a bag of chips, some candies and some chocolate cookies.
3 I dated a cute girl last night.
4 Go over the crosswalk and walk along the sidewalk till you come to the pharmacy.

Now practise the dialogues in pairs.

5. What was that?

Use one of these phrases in response to something the student next to you says in his/her own language.

I'm sorry, what was that?
What was that again?
Can you say that again, please?
I'm sorry, I don't understand.

The other student should repeat what he/she said, but this time in English.

6. What do they want?

Write down in *British* English what these Americans want.

1 __________ 2 __________ 3 __________

4 __________ 5 __________ 6 __________

7. Ask a friend

What are you doing	after school? tonight? tomorrow? next weekend?

STEP THREE Homework

I don't mind homework on weekdays – not *so* much, anyway. When I get back from school I know it's got to be done and that's that. It's homework at weekends that really gets me down.

On Friday evenings there's no problem. I can look forward to the whole weekend and there's no need to even think about homework – yet. But then on Saturday morning I start debating the question 'Shall I or shan't I?' meaning 'Shall I do my homework today and get it out of the way, or shall I leave it till Sunday?' The debate goes on for most of the day. By six in the evening I give up trying to persuade myself. There's no real necessity to do it till the next day, after all.

So that leaves Sunday. When I first wake up I think, 'Fantastic, I don't have to go to school.' But then it suddenly comes back to me – I've still got to do my homework. The whole day goes flat. And for the rest of Sunday it seems to hang over me, like a grey cloud.

The funny thing is that when I eventually get round to doing it, late on Sunday evening, of course, I find out, too late, that it's not half as bad as I imagined. It's practically ruined the whole weekend but it needn't have. It was only homework, after all.

Jessica Walters, 5C

8. When does she say it?

Choose between:

a weekday
Friday evening
Saturday morning
Saturday evening
Sunday morning
Sunday evening

1 Oh well, I haven't got any choice left now!
2 I can forget about it completely now.
3 Maybe I will, maybe I won't.
4 It's too late to start now. But there's still tomorrow.
5 I wish I could just forget about it, but I can't.
6 I'll finish it before supper as usual.

9. There's no need to . . .

Think of sentences beginning like this:

At the weekend	there's no need to . . . I don't need to . . . I needn't . . .

Compare your sentences with other students'.

10. Write sentences

Write five sentences like this:

I have to ______ on weekdays but I don't have to at weekends.

Example: I have to *get up early* on weekdays but I don't have to at weekends.

Then ask a friend about the things he/she has to do.

Example: *Do you have to get up early on weekdays too?*

11. Ask a friend

Ask him/her

1 what time he/she gets home from school.
2 what time he/she usually does homework on weekdays.
3 if he/she ever does homework on Friday evenings.
4 what he/she usually does on Saturday mornings.
5 if he/she usually leaves homework until Sunday.

STEP FOUR *Graffiti*

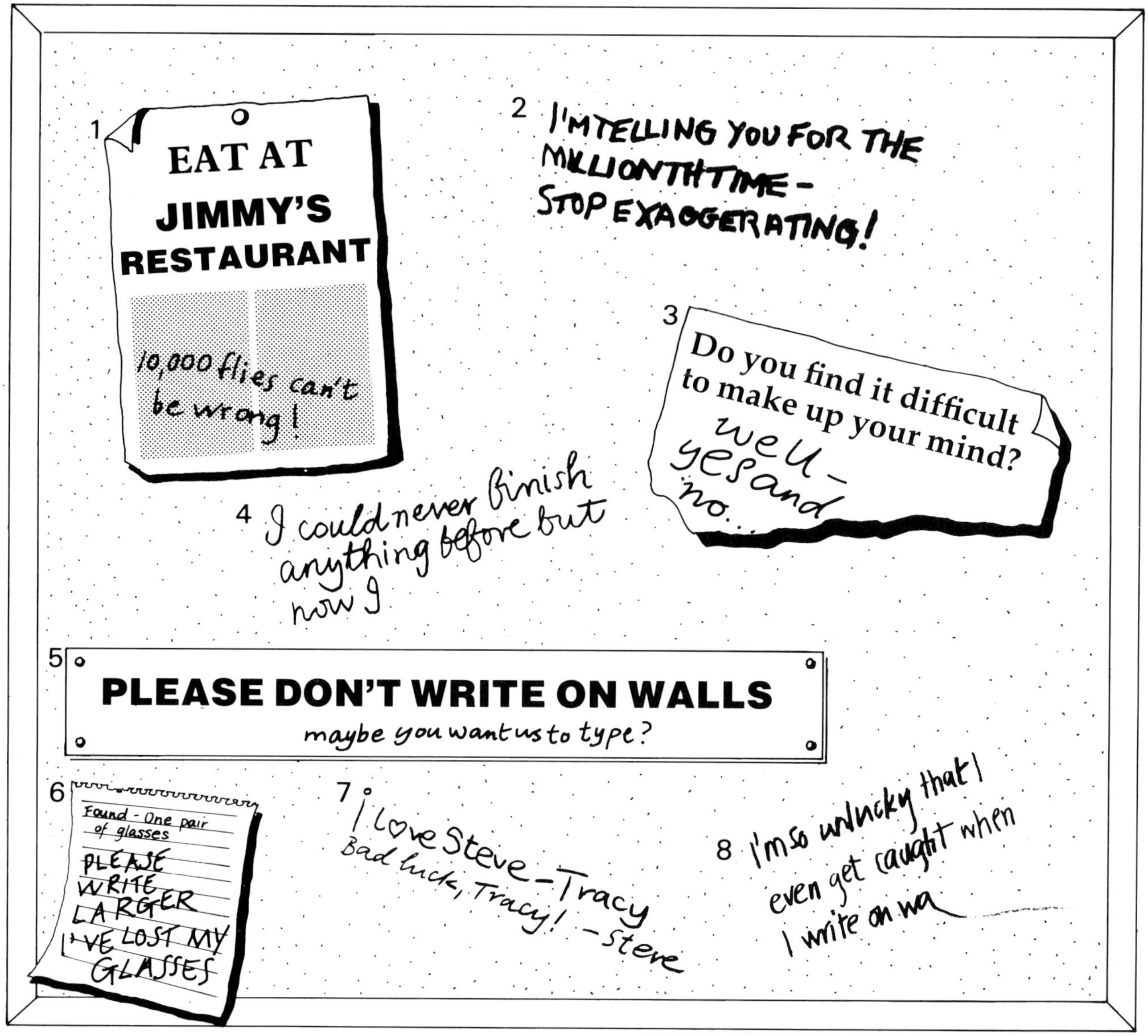

12. Reading comprehension

1 What's wrong with Jimmy's restaurant?
2 How does the 'writer' himself exaggerate?
3 Why does the 'writer' answer both 'yes' and 'no'?
4 Why does the 'writer' stop in the middle of a sentence?
5 Why is the 'writer's' suggestion absurd?
6 Why does the 'writer' want the notice to be larger?
7 How does Steve feel about Tracy?
8 Why did the 'writer' stop writing in the middle of a word? What was the word?

13. Listening comprehension

Listen to the person on the tape reading these examples of graffiti and fill in the missing words.

1 Don't write on this bus shelter.
 – *If the* __(1)__ *were on time we* __(2)__ *need to.*
2 __(3)__ enjoy the day more if it __(4)__ later.
3 When I __(5)__ I shall __(6)__ graffiti on the ceiling.
4 Eight out of __(7)__ ten men shave with an __(8)__ razor.
 – *What do the other two do with it?*
5 You can tell a British workman __(9)__ his hands – __(10)__ always in his pockets!
6 (Notice in maternity hospital) The first three __(11)__ of life can be the most __(12)__.
 – *The last three minutes are* __(13)__ *risky* __(14)__*!*

14. Writing

Add to or finish these in your own words.

1 Eat at Jimmy's restaurant!
2 Please don't write on walls.
3 I love Steve – Tracy.
4 I'm so unlucky that . . .
5 You can tell a British workman by . . .
6 Eight out of every ten . . .
7 When I grow up I shall . . .
8 I'd enjoy the day more if . . .

15. Discussion

1 Why do you think people write graffiti on walls?
2 'Historians of the future will be more interested in our graffiti than in our books.' Do you think this is true?

Grammar summary

He is	the tallest	student in the class.

<table>
<tr><td rowspan="3">Girls</td><td rowspan="2">are</td><td colspan="2">taller</td><td rowspan="3">than boys.</td></tr>
<tr><td>more
less</td><td>intelligent</td></tr>
<tr><td>grow</td><td>more
less</td><td>quickly</td></tr>
</table>

<table>
<tr><td>I
You
We
They</td><td>have to
need to</td><td rowspan="2">go.</td></tr>
<tr><td>He
She
It</td><td>has to
needs to</td></tr>
</table>

<table>
<tr><td>I
You
We</td><td>don't</td><td rowspan="2">have to
need to</td><td rowspan="4">do the homework.</td></tr>
<tr><td rowspan="2">They
He
She</td><td>doesn't</td></tr>
<tr><td colspan="2">needn't</td></tr>
<tr><td colspan="3">There's no need to</td></tr>
</table>

4

STEP ONE *The fourth bedroom*

A: Good morning.
B: Good morning.
A: We've come to see your house.
B: My house?
A: Yes, it's for sale, isn't it?
B: Oh, yes, it's for sale, all right.
A: Well . . . um . . . can we come in?
B: Come in?
A: Yes, may we come in and look around?
B: Oh, yes, I suppose so.
C: It's very nice.
B: What is?
C: This room.
B: Do you think so?
C: Yes, I do. It's just big enough but not too big. Do you know what I mean?
A: And I like the kitchen. It's quite modern, isn't it?
B: Modern?
A: Yes, these units and cupboards, I mean.
B: Oh, yes, those. My husband made those.
C: Your husband?
B: Yes. He's upstairs, of course. He can't come down, you understand.
C: Oh, yes, we understand.
A: Well, could we look upstairs?
B: Yes, if you've got enough time.
C: How many bedrooms did you say there were?
B: I didn't say.
C: Well, how many are there?
B: There are three.
A: That's funny. The agents said there were four. And three's not enough.
B: There were four. But there aren't any longer.
A: How do you mean?
B: Well, my husband's in one of them, so that only leaves three.
A: Yes, but surely . . .
B: No, it's out of the question. He'd never agree to leave his room. But you can look at it, if you like. It's this door here, on the left.
C: Oh, no, we wouldn't like to disturb him.
B: It's all right. You won't, I promise. It's too late.
A: But . . . but . . .
B: You see, I said you wouldn't disturb him. You couldn't disturb him. Not now, not any longer . . .

1. True or false?

1 The agents sent the couple to look at the house.
2 The woman in the house didn't know it was for sale.
3 The kitchen was very big.
4 The house was on one floor.
5 The kitchen was upstairs.
6 The house had only three bedrooms.
7 The couple wanted a four-bedroom house.
8 The woman's husband was upstairs.
9 It wasn't possible to disturb her husband.

STEP TWO

2. Ask permission

Use: can may could

Examples: Can *I come in?*
May *I ask you a question?*
Could *I see you for a minute?*

Think of other examples, and then practise them with a friend, like this:

– *Can I borrow your pen?*
– *Yes, of course.*
– *May I have a look at your paper?*
– *No, I'm afraid not. I'm reading it myself.*

3. What do they say?

In the following pictures one person asks permission:

Can I . . . ?
May I . . . ?
Could I . . . ?

The other answers: Yes, of course *or* No, I'm afraid not.

Example:

Can I share your umbrella? – No, I'm afraid not.

Now fill in the speech bubbles in the following pictures.

4. Dialogue

Work in pairs.

Possible buyer	Owner of house
Explain who you are and why you have come.	Invite him/her in.
Explain why you are looking for a new house.	Describe the house.
Ask how many bedrooms there are.	Tell him/her.
Say the agent said one more.	Explain the mistake.
Say you are not interested in the house, and explain why.	Apologise for the mistake.
Say goodbye.	Say goodbye.

5. Listening

Listen to the voices on the tape and write which room each person is in.

6. Is it big enough?

Write sentences about the following things.

Use:
- not big enough
- just big enough
- too big

Example: *My bedroom is not big enough.*

1 Your house or flat
2 Your class
3 Your classroom
4 Your shoes
5 Your family

STEP THREE *Odd facts about animals*

Bees communicate by dancing. Whenever a bee finds some flowers with a lot of nectar, it flies straight back to the hive and does a strange kind of dance. The steps and rhythm of the dance tell the other bees exactly where to go, and even the colour of the flowers.

The muscles which an alligator uses to open its mouth are very, very weak. However hard the alligator tries to open its mouth, you can keep it shut with only one hand. But, whatever happens, don't try to hold an alligator's mouth *open*. The muscles which close it are fantastically strong!

However quiet you are, or however dark it is, a rattlesnake will always know you are coming. But it doesn't hear or see whoever is coming – it *feels* him! Between its eyes and nostrils there are cells which can feel a temperature difference of only .00055 degrees centigrade – that is, a mouse's body heat 15 centimetres away!

Whenever a male Toci Toci beetle wants to find a female to mate with, he taps on a stone with his back legs. Wherever she is, up to a distance of five kilometres away, the female can hear the sound. But a sensitive microphone, a few centimetres away, 'hears' nothing!

Whatever you do, don't get too near the Golden Arrow poison frog of Colombia, South America. One millionth of a gram of its poison is enough to kill you! The poison from the skin of just one frog is enough to kill 2,200 people!

7. What are the questions?

Example: How *do bees* communicate?
By dancing.

1 What . . . bee . . . nectar?
It flies straight back to the hive.

2 How . . . male . . . female?
By tapping on a stone.

3 How far . . . female . . . male?
Five kilometres away.

4 How . . . alligator's . . . shut?
It's very easy.

5 How . . . rattlesnake . . . coming?
It feels you.

6 Where . . . cells . . . difference?
Between its eyes and nostrils.

7 How much . . . kill . . .?
One millionth of a gram.

8. Make sentences

The poison of the golden arrow poison frog will kill you		happens.
Don't try to hold open an alligator's mouth	wherever	it is.
The female Toci Toci beetle can hear the male	however	small the quantity.
A rattlesnake knows when you are coming	whenever	they find nectar.
Bees communicate with other bees in the hive	whatever	he is.
The other bees can then find the nectar		he wants to find a female.
A male Toci Toci beetle taps on a stone		quiet you are.

9. Writing

Complete these sentences with your own ideas.

1 Whenever I . . .
2 However hard I . . .
3 Whatever I . . .
4 Wherever I . . .
5 Whoever I . . .

STEP FOUR *Self-help in Pasco County*

This is a leaflet sent to all the people living in Regency Park, Pasco County, Florida, USA. Before you read it, look at these questions.
1 Why does Regency Park need a Neighborhood Watch Patrol?
2 What does a member of the patrol do?
3 How do you become a member of the patrol?
Now read the leaflet. By the end of it you should know the answers to the three questions above. Answer them orally.

JOIN YOUR LOCAL

NEIGHBORHOOD WATCH PATROL

We need your help *now*!

Give only two hours a week of your time.

Help us cut down on crime *now* – before it happens . . .

Help make our homes and families safer thru this great community effort.

We work closely with the Pasco County Sheriff's Department.

We also offer rescue help in weather emergencies to shut-ins and people unable to drive.

We ask both renters and home owners to join us.

The more members we have, the longer hours of protection and safety we can offer.

No fees are payable – only your time and your car are needed.

We are a non-profit organization relying entirely on voluntary donations.

For more details call
Gordon Carroll at 863-6758.
Don't delay – join your friends and neighbors.
Do it today.

WE NEED YOU!

Now read the leaflet again carefully. If possible, work out the meaning of new words or, if you can't, look them up in a dictionary.

10. Reading comprehension

Are these statements true or false?

1 A member of the Neighborhood Watch Patrol works more than ten hours a month.
2 The only job of the Neighborhood Watch Patrol is to cut down on crime.
3 Some houses in Regency Park are rented.
4 If the Neighborhood Watch Patrol gets more members, it will work for longer than two hours a week.
5 It costs nothing to become a member of the Neighborhood Watch Patrol.
6 The Sheriff's Department pays for some of the cost of the Neighborhood Watch Patrol.

11. Listening comprehension

Listen to this conversation and fill in the information needed for the identification card.

12. Writing

You want new members for a club or organisation in your school or area. Write a leaflet giving the necessary information and explaining why you want new members.

13. Discussion

1 Would a Neighborhood Watch Patrol be a good idea in your area?
2 'The richer a country is, the more crime it has.' Do you agree?

Grammar summary

It's	(not)	too small.

It's	(not)	big enough.

There	are	(n't)	enough rooms.

There	is	(n't)	enough money.

5

STEP ONE *Mother and daughter (1) – the mother's story*

I started to worry when Kathy wasn't on the 5.30 bus. 'She must have missed it', I thought, 'but why?'

I was alone in the house. My husband was away on business. I was afraid of what might have happened to Kathy. Why hadn't she phoned? 'She may have gone home with her best friend, Elaine,' I thought. So I phoned Elaine's mother.

'No, I'm sorry, she isn't here. She might be with another friend,' she suggested.

I phoned some of Kathy's friends. None of them had seen her since she left school as usual at 4 o'clock. 'Where can she be?' I asked myself over and over again.

I started to cry. I couldn't stop myself thinking about what could have happened to her. I sat by the phone, waiting for it to ring.

Finally, at ten to nine, Elaine's mother rang. 'She's with us,' she said. I felt as though an enormous weight had been lifted from me, as though I was walking on air.

I drove round to collect her. She was very quiet and just looked at me coldly. In the car she was silent. She must have been sorry, but she didn't say anything. I wanted to be angry, to tell her how worried I'd been. But I was afraid she would only see the anger and not the love I felt.

So I decided to just be nice. She answered all my questions, but very calmly and coolly. She must have realised that I'd gone through a lot of pain and worry because of her, but she showed no sign of it.

When we got home, we watched television for a bit and behaved as though nothing had happened. It was forgotten, pushed away out of sight. She may remember that evening. She might even regret it. But she's never said anything. Not a word!

1. Make sentences

Kathy's mother	was	some of Kathy's friends.
	phoned	by the phone.
	started	as though she was walking on air.
	sat	round to collect her.
	drove	to be nice.
	wanted	to cry.
	decided	alone in the house.
	felt	to be angry.

2. She must have missed the bus

What went through Kathy's mother's head? Write sentences.

Kathy	may might must	be have	. . .

Compare your sentences in class.

3. What do you think?

Should Kathy's mother have: waited for Kathy to ring her?
guessed she was at a friend's house?
been more angry when she first saw her?
told her how worried she'd been?

Answer: *Yes, she should* or *No, she shouldn't.*

Give reasons for your answers. Compare your answers with other students'.

STEP TWO Mother and daughter (2) – the daughter's story

After school I met Jane. She'd borrowed a cassette of mine, so I went home with her to collect it. I didn't feel like going home anyway. I shouldn't really say this, but my mother and I get on each other's nerves a bit, so I try to keep out of her way.

Jane and I talked for a long time. Then I suddenly realised I'd missed both buses so I'd have to walk home.

'My mum'll go mad,' I said. 'I must phone and tell her where I am.'

'But we haven't got a phone,' Jane said, 'and anyway, why should you? She's going to be annoyed anyway, so it doesn't really matter how late you are.'

That sounded reasonable so we went on talking for a bit.

On the way home I passed Elaine's house, so I had to go in to see her.

'Your mum's going mad. She's been phoning everyone. You'll be in real trouble when you get home. I think you ought to phone her.'

'Oh, no!' What was I going to say to her? Did I really have to phone her?

Then Elaine's mother came in and told me I didn't have to because she'd already rung my mother.

Ten minutes later she arrived. I expected her to be furious with me. But instead she just stood quietly at the front door and thanked Elaine's mother for phoning.

I knew I should apologise. But I was angry. Why had she told everyone she was worried? Now she was acting as if nothing had happened!

In the car I didn't see why I should talk about it. It was clear that she didn't really care about me. That hurt me more than anything.

Parents ought to love their children – so why doesn't my mother love me?

4. Ask Kathy

Complete the questions with the right question word and then answer them. Work in pairs.

1 ______ did you go home with?
2 ______ do you sometimes try to keep out of your mother's way?
3 ______ did you talk to Jane about?
4 ______ didn't you phone your mother?
5 ______ did you go in and see on your way home?
6 ______ did Elaine's mother tell you?
7 ______ did your mother arrive?
8 ______ did she behave when she arrived?
9 ______ did you feel?
10 ______ did you think on the way home?

5. Discussion

Should Kathy have: gone home immediately after school?
rung her mother?
guessed how worried her mother was?
apologised to her mother?

Discuss your answers and the reasons for them.
What would *you* have done if you had been in Kathy's situation?

6. What do you think?

Write sentences.

Kathy Kathy's mother	should(n't) have . . . ought(n't) to have . . .

Mothers Daughters/Sons	should(n't) . . . have to . . . must(n't) . . .

Compare your sentences with other students'.

7. A dialogue

Read *the mother's story* and *the daughter's story* again and then write the dialogue in the car on the way home, between Kathy and her mother. Act out your dialogues in pairs.

STEP THREE Megamouth

In 1976 the US research ship *Achilles* was anchored off Hawaii. When the time came to move on, the anchor chain, which was nearly 500 metres long, felt rather heavy. The captain ordered his crew to keep on pulling. Eventually, the reason for the extra weight broke the surface of the water. An extremely large fish – some kind of shark – was caught in the anchor chain. With much difficulty, they killed it and pulled it on board. It was 4.5 metres long, weighed 750 kilos – and was extremely ugly.

The biologists on board looked through every book they had. But none had any reference to a shark like this. The crew named it Megamouth.

Since then, scientists have agreed that Megamouth is a completely new species. No other Megamouths have ever been found, before or since. It is quite unique.

But perhaps that's not so surprising. Very few fishermen have lines 500 metres long – the depth at which Megamouth lives all its life in almost total darkness.

And in case someone thinks of making a horror movie with Megamouth as its star, its 236 teeth are, in fact, almost completely harmless. They act only as a kind of sieve. The thick red 'soup' found in Megamouth's stomach was not from human victims, but from millions of very tiny shrimps!

8. Interview the captain of the *Achilles*

Complete the questions and then answer them. Work in pairs.

1 What sort of ship ______ the *Achilles*?
2 Where ______ it anchored?
3 How long ______ the anchor?
4 How long ______ Megamouth?
5 How much ______ it weigh?
6 What ______ it look like?
7 What ______ special about Megamouth?
8 What ______ it eat?
9 How many teeth ______ it have?
10 ______ it dangerous?

9. A dialogue

Complete the following dialogue between two members of the crew of the *Achilles*, just before they catch Megamouth.

A: How long is the anchor chain?
B: . . . 500 metres.
A: . . . heavy!
B: . . . don't understand . . .
A: . . . fish . . . anchor chain.
B: . . . shark.
A: . . . on board.
B: . . . kill . . .!
A: . . . long . . .?
B: . . . 4.5 metres . . .
A: . . . heavy . . .?
B: . . . 750 . . .
A: . . . ugly!
B: . . . Megamouth!

Now practise the dialogue in pairs.

10. What are they like?

Describe the things on the left using one of the words on the right, plus a suitable adjective.

Megamouth	very
sharks	completely
Hawaii	almost
horror movies	extremely
shrimps	quite
Megamouth's teeth	rather
fish soup	incredibly

Examples:
Megamouth was very heavy.
Megamouth was extremely ugly.
Megamouth was absolutely unique.

11. Listening

Listen and fill in the missing information, using this table.

Depth at which it lives	Weight	Length	Number of teeth	Food

STEP FOUR *The big fish*

This is part of a story called The Old Man and the Sea *by the American writer Ernest Hemingway. Before you read it, look at these questions.*

1 Is the old man alone?
2 Why does it take so long to catch the fish?
3 Does he kill the fish in the end?
4 How does he feel at the end?

Now read the passage. By the end of it you should know the answers to the four questions above. Answer them orally.

(Santiago, an old Cuban fisherman, is out at sea after going for 84 days without catching anything. Now he has hooked a big fish which tows his boat along for 36 hours. On the second day the fish begins to circle.)

It was on the third turn that he saw the fish first.

He saw him first as a dark shadow that took so long to pass under the boat that he could not believe its length.

'No,' he said. 'He can't be that big.'

But he was that big and at the end of this circle he came to the surface only thirty yards away and the man saw his tail out of the water. It was higher than a big scythe blade and a very pale lavender above the dark blue water.

The old man was sweating now but from something else besides the sun. On each calm placid turn the fish made he was gaining line and he was sure that in two turns more he would have a chance to get the harpoon in.

But I must get him close, close, close, he thought. I mustn't try for the head. I must get the heart.

'Be calm and strong, old man,' he said.

(But it takes him much longer than he expects to pull in the fish.)

'Fish', the old man said. 'Fish, you are going to have to die anyway. Do you have to kill me too?'

That way nothing is accomplished, he thought. His mouth was too dry to speak but he could not reach for the water now. I must get him alongside this time, he thought. I am not good for many more turns. Yes you are, he told himself. You're good for ever.

You are killing me, fish, the old man thought. But you have a right to. Never have I seen a greater, or a more beautiful, or a calmer or more noble thing than you, brother. Come on and kill me. I do not care who kills who.

(But eventually the fish does come close enough.)

He took all his pain and what was left of his strength and his long gone pride and he put it against the fish's agony and the fish came over on to his side and swam gently on his side, his bill almost touching the planking of the skiff, and started to pass the boat, long, deep, wide, silver and barred with purple and interminable in the water.

The old man dropped the line and put his foot on it and lifted the harpoon as high as he could and drove it down with all his strength, and more strength he had just summoned, into the fish's side just behind the great chest fin that rose high in the air to the altitude of the man's chest. He felt the iron go in and he leaned on it and drove it further and then pushed all his weight after it.

Then the fish came alive, with his death in him, and rose high out of the water showing all his great length and width and all his power and his beauty. He seemed to hang in the air above the old man in the skiff. Then he fell into the water with a crash that sent spray over the old man and over all of the skiff. The old man took two turns of the harpoon line around the bitt in the bow and laid his head on his hands.

'Keep my head clear,' he said against the wood of the bow. 'I am a tired old man. But I have killed this fish which is my brother.'

12. Reading comprehension

Read the passage again carefully. A number of words are probably new to you. In many cases, however, you should be able to guess their meaning from other things in the sentence. For example, do you think a scythe is (a) a kind of tree, (b) a kind of tool, or (c) a kind of animal? (The word 'blade' should help you.) Now guess the meaning of these words:

lavender (a) a shadow
(b) a sail
(c) a colour

a skiff (a) a boat
(b) the crew of a boat
(c) the sail of a boat

a bitt (a) a mast
(b) part of a boat for tying lines or cables to
(c) a metal ring

the bow (a) part of a ship or boat
(b) part of a fish
(c) part of your arm

13. Answer the questions

1 Why was the fish swimming in circles?
2 What did the fish look like?
3 Why did the fish come nearer and nearer to the boat?
4 Why was it important to get the fish very close before he used the harpoon?
5 Why was the old man so weak?
6 Which part of the fish did the harpoon enter?
7 What happened when he harpooned the fish?
8 Why did he call the fish 'my brother'?

14. Listening comprehension

Listen to the tape and decide which statements are true and which are false.

15. Writing

What happens next? Write the next paragraph of the story using your imagination.

16. Discussion

1 Do you think the old man should have let the fish go?
2 'It is wrong to kill an animal for any reason other than self-defence.' Do you agree?

Grammar summary

I You He She It We You They	could may might must (can't)	be with a friend. have missed the bus.

<table>
<tr><td rowspan="2">I
You
He
She
It
We
You
They</td><td>must (n't)</td><td>phone.</td></tr>
<tr><td>should (n't)
ought (n't) to</td><td>phone.
have phoned.</td></tr>
</table>

6

STEP ONE *On the right track*

Jimmy Moomba is 69 and one of the last Aboriginal trackers in Australia. He learned his job when he was only a small boy. By the age of five, he could track animals like emus, wildcats and kangaroos in the desert. As a man, Jimmy worked on cattle and sheep stations all over South Australia.

But later on the police began to employ Jimmy whenever they wanted to track someone who had got lost in the bush, or an escaped prisoner. He became famous when he 'followed' a dangerous murderer, Charles Tompkins, who had escaped from prison and run off into the desert.

There were footprints everywhere, from prison officers and policemen. But Jimmy soon became interested in some particular footprints and started to track them. The policemen couldn't understand why, but nevertheless followed him off into the desert in the 40° heat.

After a few kilometres, Jimmy wasn't able to see the tracks any longer. The ground was too stony. The policemen thought he'd have to give up. 'Let's just go on a bit, in this direction,' Jimmy said. And, sure enough, five kilometres further on he found the tracks again.

'When you can't see a track, you have to be able to *think* like the man you're following.'

As he continued to follow the tracks, Jimmy gave the policemen behind him a running commentary:

'He's carrying a bag in his right hand . . . He crawled under this fence . . . He scratched his left leg on that piece of wire. There's some blood on it, and it's not quite dry. That means we're about three hours behind him . . . You see this half-eaten apple? He threw it away about two hours ago.'

As they got further out into the bush, the policemen kept close to Jimmy. 'When he's tracking,' one of them said, 'he doesn't hear you even if you yell after him because you're lost. He just keeps on going!'

An hour later Jimmy started chuckling to himself: 'This man knows we're following him, and he believes he can trick me – just by walking backwards. But he doesn't know that Jimmy Moomba is following him! He doesn't understand – he can't escape from me. But he seems to be tiring now – he's walking more and more slowly.'

Soon Jimmy started getting nervous. 'He's very close now. I want you to get the dogs and your guns. I'm waiting back here. I think he's probably sleeping up in a tree.'

Jimmy then waited while two policemen with dogs and guns went on in the direction Jimmy pointed. Sure enough, less than 100 metres further on, they found Tompkins asleep in a tree. On his left leg there was a scratch!

Jimmy stayed behind. He didn't even want to look at the man he'd been following for so long.

1. What are they doing?

Describe what is happening in each picture. Then put the pictures in the order they happen in the text.

1

2

3

4

5

6

7

STEP TWO

2. Questions and answers

Complete the questions and answers. Use the present tense.
Then ask and answer in pairs.

Example: he/walk/more slowly?
tired
Why is he walking more slowly?
Because he's getting tired.

1 Jimmy/look for footprints?
escaped prisoner
2 Tompkins/eat an apple?
hungry
3 he/walk backwards?
the police
4 Jimmy/wait behind?
nervous
5 the police/carry guns?
escaped murderer
6 the police/go/towards those trees?
Tompkins/tree

3. Make true sentences

Jimmy Moomba	is(not) able to was(not) able to	track animals when he was only 5. get jobs on cattle or sheep stations. think like the man he's following. see footprints if the ground is stony. work when the temperature is 40°. tell how far he is behind the person he's following. look at the man he'd been following.

4. Write sentences

When I was young I	was able to wasn't able to	. . .

When I leave school	I'll be able to I won't be able to	. . .

5. Complete the sentences

Complete the following sentences using the present continuous or the present simple.

Jimmy Moomba ([1] track) an escaped murderer. He ([2] give) the policeman behind him a running commentary.

'I ([3] think) he ([4] carry) a bag in his right hand. You ([5] see) this apple? – that ([6] mean) we're about two hours behind him. He ([7] know) the police ([8] follow) him, but he ([9] not know) Jimmy Moomba ([10] track) him! He ([11] walk) more slowly now. He ([12] seem) to be tiring. I ([13] think) we ([14] be) close to him now. I ([15] get) nervous. I ([16] not want) to go on. He ([17] wait) for us in those trees.'

6. A newspaper report

Write the newspaper report of how the police, with Jimmy Moomba's help, captured Charles Tompkins.

7. Wanted!

Five people are wanted by the South Australian police. Listen to the tape and write the correct number under each picture.

STEP THREE *Animal stories*

LOST PROPERTY

A 1.3-METRE, 38-kilo porpoise was found in the men's toilet on Glasgow Central Station yesterday.

The toilet cleaner who first discovered it thought it was a dolphin. But an expert from the Kelvingrove Park Museum later identified it as a six-year-old male porpoise.

Nobody has yet claimed it from the Railway Lost Property Office, or explained how it came to be in the toilet. A British Rail spokesman commented, "We've had a lot of heavy rain recently and some flooding, but this is ridiculous!"

REST IN PEACE

MR PERCY GRUNDY (62), of Elstead near Farnham, Kent, is the owner of a 40-hectare farm. He is also the owner of a ten-year-old chestnut horse called Roger. Roger, for reasons only known to himself, likes to sleep on his back, with his legs in the air, his eyes shut and his mouth open.

So many passing motorists have telephoned the local police that Mr Grundy has put a large sign up on the gate of Roger's field. It says: THIS HORSE IS NOT DEAD!

8. Write sentences

Write sentences beginning like this:

A	10-year-old 62-year-old 40-hectare 38-kilo 1.3-metre	farmer farm horse porpoise	. . .

Compare your sentences with other students'.

9. Descriptions

Example: *a six-year-old horse*

1 42 kilos

2 60 years old

3 2 hectares

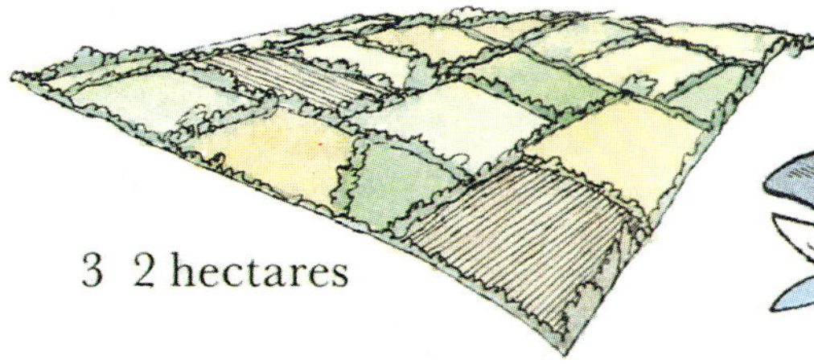

4 3 metres

10. Found!

Write the advertisement which British Rail put in the Glasgow Herald to try and find the owner of the porpoise.

Include information about where it was found, its length, weight, age, etc.

11. A conversation

Write the telephone conversation between a passing motorist and a policeman, in which the motorist reports that he has seen a dead horse.

Act out the dialogue in pairs.

12. Ask a friend

Ask if he/she has ever:

- seen a porpoise.
- seen a dolphin.
- been to Glasgow.
- been to a museum.
- lost anything on a train.
- found any lost property.
- owned a horse.
- ridden a horse.
- seen a horse asleep.
- seen a horse asleep with its legs in the air.

STEP FOUR ***Burr-ee-toh***

This menu is from a typical American 'Mexican' restaurant.
Before you read it, look at these questions.

1 Is the food in this restaurant always 'hot' and spicy?
2 Can you only buy non-alcoholic drinks in this restaurant?
3 If you want to eat cheaply, when should you go to a Taco Bravo restaurant?
4 Do you have to eat your food in the restaurant?

Now read the menu. By the end you should know the answers to the questions above. Answer them orally.

MEET TACO BRAVO. AND MEET WHAT YOU EAT.

First, a word about our sauces . . .
Mexican food doesn't have to be hot to be good. It's all in the sauce . . . "Mild" is like salad dressing. "Medium" is like Italian sauce. "Extra Hot" has pip and pow. "Jalapeno" is hot, hot and good, good, with a definite pepper flavor. "El Scorcho" is pure pain for some, pure pleasure for others. If you want a little extra sauce, just ask. There's no extra charge.

Guacamole (GWAK-AH-MOLE-EE)
A favorite avocado chip dip south of the border. A blend of avocado with onions, garlic and seasonings topped with tomatoes on a bed of lettuce. Served with a generous helping of crisp corn tortilla chips.

The Taco Bravo Taco (TAH-KOH)
● Beef ● Bean ● Combination ● Soft Taco
Beef or Refried Beans or a Combination. All with lettuce, cheese, and tomato served on either a crisp U-shaped corn tortilla (frito shell) or in a soft corn tortilla. Your choice of five sauces. Or no sauces.

Taco Bravo Burrito (BURR-EE-TOH)
● Beef ● Bean ● Combination
A big wheat flour tortilla filled with beef, beef and beans or all beans. Plus cheddar cheese, lettuce and your choice of seasoning. Want fresh onions? Just ask! No charge.

Mexican Rice
We start with the best long-grain rice we can get. Then we add three different vegetables (no tomato sauce) and spices. The result: A delicious combination of individual grains of rice and distinctive flavors.

And a whole lot of ways to wet your whistle . . .
Draft beer, home made sangria and excellent house wines are available in most locations. We offer a hearty burgundy, chablis and vin rose in generous portions. Coke,® Sprite,® Tab,® Fanta® Root Beer and Grape, Lemonade, Milk, Lipton pre-sweetened Ice Tea with lemon.

Take us home
Taco Bravo Takout: We'll fix it for you to go, or we'll sell you the fixin's to do it yourself. We've even got drive-thru windows in some locations. And in all locations, we've got great prices!
Slight service charge on some takeout items.

Special days twice a week
MONDAY Three beef tacos at a very special price. After 4 PM.
WEDNESDAY Something Completely Different Day. A different special all day each Wednesday. A special price for every special.

We cater, too!
Ask the manager. We're very good. And very, very inexpensive!
When you say "Taco"...Say "Bravo" from lunch to the late evening every day except Thanksgiving and Christmas.

TACO BRAVO DINNERS

Real Mexican meals, real gringo deals!

Read the menu again carefully. If possible, work out the meaning of new words or, if you can't, look them up in a dictionary.

13. Reading comprehension

1 Which is the hottest sauce you can choose?
2 How much extra do you have to pay if you have onions with your 'burrito'?
3 Do you get any meat with 'Mexican rice'?
4 Which sign do you look for if you want to eat without getting out of your car?
5 If you're having a party, who should you talk to at the Taco Bravo restaurant?
6 Which days of the year is the restaurant not open?

14. Listening comprehension

Listen to the tape. You are a waiter at the Taco Bravo restaurant. Write down what the four people on one table order to eat and drink.

15. Writing

Write part of a menu from a restaurant which specialises in food which is typical for your country. Describe the food in a way which is similar to that in the Taco Bravo menu.

16. Discussion

1 Do you think you would enjoy a Taco Bravo meal?
2 'Quite soon, the whole world will be eating the same things.' Do you think this is true?

Grammar summary

<table>
<tr><td rowspan="2">He</td><td colspan="2">can ('t)
could (n't)</td><td rowspan="2">track criminals.</td></tr>
<tr><td>is (n't)
was (n't)</td><td>able to</td></tr>
</table>

The porpoise weighed	38 kilos.
It was a	38-kilo porpoise.

7

STEP ONE *The history of the hot dog*

Back in 1900, a man was trying to sell sausages in the streets of New York. He boiled them and then kept them hot in a tank of hot water. Nobody was very interested until he started to shout, 'Get your hot dachshund sausages here!' (A dachshund is a long, thin, brown dog which looks something like a sausage.) As a result he sold many more of his sausages.

A newspaper reporter took a photograph, for a story in his paper, of the sausage seller holding up one of his sausages. But he wasn't sure how to spell 'dachshund', so he called it a 'hot dog' instead. And that's how the name started.

The same salesman lent a pair of white gloves to his customers to hold the hot sausages with. But somebody forgot to give him back the gloves. So he went to a baker and asked him to make him some long pieces of bread to hold the hot dog in.

This was such a perfect combination that it has remained unchanged ever since!

The history of Coca-Cola

Coca-Cola was originally invented by John Pemberton, a pharmacist in Atlanta, Georgia. In 1886, he made up a new kind of medicine to cure tiredness and headaches.

But it tasted revolting, and as a result almost nobody wanted to buy it. In the first year, Pemberton only made $50 from it!

Then a businessman bought the recipe and advertised it, not as a medicine but as a refreshing drink. All he did was mix it with water and carbon dioxide! It worked. Everybody wanted to buy it and in only a few years Coca-Cola became the national drink of the United States. The shape of the famous bottle was invented in 1916.

During the Second World War American soldiers drank three million bottles of Coca-Cola – a day! They therefore helped to spread the name and the taste for 'Coke' all over the world. Today, nearly 300 million bottles are drunk every day, in 155 different countries.

Anybody can try to make a drink which tastes *something* like Coca-Cola. Chemists say that it consists almost entirely of carbonated water and sugar. But nobody outside the Coca-Cola company has yet discovered what the 'magic' extra ingredients are, and very few people – only seven, in fact – have ever known the secret formula of Coca-Cola. Only two of them are alive today, so they never travel on the same plane!

STEP TWO

1. Make true sentences

He called them 'dachshunds' because a dachshund looks The newspaper reporter took a picture of The salesman lent gloves to customers until The pharmacist made only \$50 because It's possible for The formula for Coca-Cola is so secret that	somebody anybody nobody something	like a sausage. was interested in his sausages. forgot to give them back. eating a hot dog. to try to make a drink similar to Coca-Cola. outside the company has ever known it. wanted to buy his medicine.

2. Results

Join the sentences. Use: so because

Example: He wasn't selling many sausages. He called them 'hot dachshunds'.
He wasn't selling many sausages so he called them 'hot dachshunds'.
He called them 'hot dachshunds' because he wasn't selling many sausages.

1 He couldn't spell 'dachshund'. He called them 'hot dogs'.
2 They got their hands dirty. He lent them gloves.
3 One customer forgot to give back the gloves. He put the sausages between two pieces of bread.
4 It tasted revolting. Nobody bought it.
5 A businessman mixed it with water and carbon dioxide. Everybody wanted to buy it.
6 American soldiers drank a lot of Coca-Cola during the Second World War. The name and taste for Coca-Cola spread.
7 The Coca-Cola company want to keep the formula secret. Only two men know the recipe for Coca-Cola.

3. Make 'of'- phrases

Make phrases from the following table and then put them into complete sentences.

Example: *long pieces of bread*
Hot dogs are usually eaten between long pieces of bread.

the streets a tank a pair a new kind the national drink the shape three million bottles	of	hot water medicine the USA New York white gloves Coca-Cola a day the famous bottle

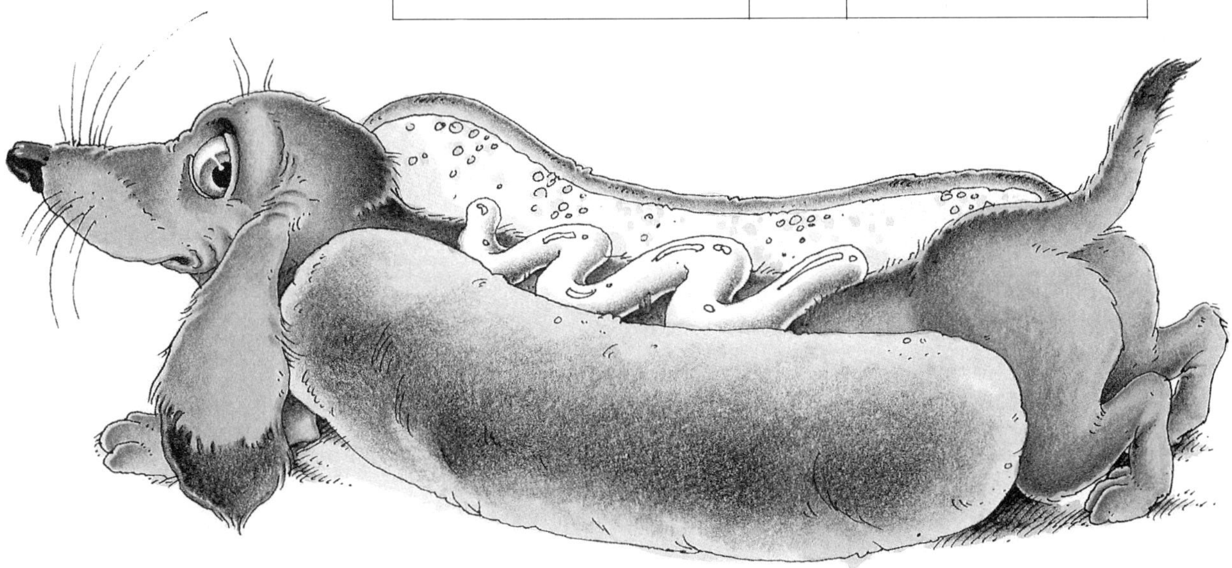

4. A slogan

Write your own slogan or advertisement for Coca-Cola. Work in groups.

5. A conversation

Write the conversation between the pharmacist and the businessman who bought the recipe from him.

6. Ingredients

Listen to the ingredients of the following things and write them down.

STEP THREE Carrot-top

I was born with a handicap. When I say this people usually just start laughing, not because they enjoy being cruel, but simply because they don't take me seriously. So what is my handicap? I was born with *red hair*. I hate it!

Before you start yawning and saying, 'So what? I don't like my funny nose', or whatever, let me explain. When people see someone with red hair, they immediately start making silly remarks like, 'Hey, Carrot-top!' And they go on making them, over and over again. I can't stand it. It wouldn't be so bad if the jokes were funny. But they never are!

And after they've finished making those sort of remarks, they change to, 'Ho ho, your face is as red as your hair', and that's when I start getting angry. I didn't use to have a temper. I think I've developed it just to satisfy people who expect it, just because I've got red hair.

I don't mind going out when it's cold and wet, but I hate going out when it's hot. In fact I dread the summer. Other people go brown, and within days they're showing me their Mediterranean tans. But I'm either a bright pink colour and covered in freckles, or I'm hiding inside, in the shade.

It's sad, but when you're young like me, all you want is to be accepted, to be normal! Quite simply, I hate being different! I suppose fat teenagers or ones with ears which stick out feel the same, but *surely* they can't feel as bad as me – the one they all call 'Carrot-top'.

7. Interview 'Carrot-top'

Ask him

1 what people do when he says he's got a handicap.
2 what people start making silly remarks about.
3 if their remarks are funny.
4 if he's got a temper.
5 if he's always had one.
6 why he dreads the summer.
7 where he spends most of the summer.
8 why he hates being different.

8. Write sentences

Complete the following sentences in any way you like.

1 I like . . .
2 I don't like . . .
3 I hate . . .
4 I can't stand . . .
5 I dread . . .

Now compare with what other students have written and ask each other questions like:

Why don't you like . . .?
Why do you hate . . .?
Why can't you stand . . .?
Why do you dread . . .?

9. Ask a friend

1 Do you know anybody with red hair? (Would they prefer their hair to be a different colour?)
2 Do people make silly remarks to him/her?
3 Do you think you've got a funny nose? (Do people make funny remarks about it?)
4 Do you ever have freckles? (Do you mind?)
5 Have you got a temper? (When do you show it?)
6 Do you dread the summer? (Why?)
7 Do you go brown easily or do you go pink first? (Do you try to go brown?)

10. A survey

Almost everybody would like to change some part of their face or body. Find out what the other students in the class are unhappy with. Ask: 'What would you like to change?'

Then compare the answers to see which parts of the body people most commonly want to change.

STEP FOUR ***Sea, sun and sand***

This short guide to some Greek islands appeared in a British newspaper. Before you read it, look at these questions.

1 What information does the guide give you about getting to the various islands?

2 What are the main differences between the two groups of islands?

3 What other information does the guide give you?

Now read the article. By the end of it you should know the answers to the three questions above. Answer them orally.

Picking your Greek Island

There are over a hundred Greek islands. The following short guide may help you to choose *your* holiday island.

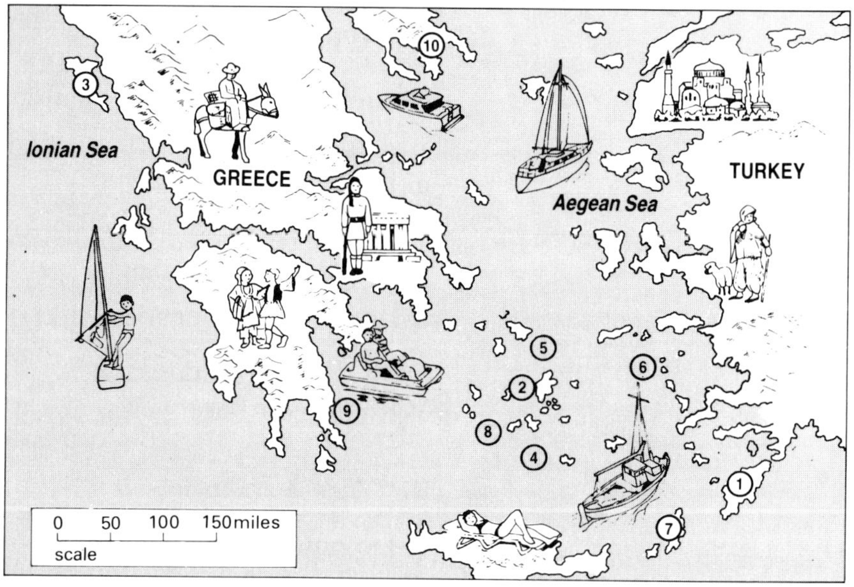

Key

A: Accessibility
- **** Direct flights from Britain
- *** Easy travel on from Athens by air/sea
- ** 4-9 hours from Athens
- * Irregular or long ferry journey

B: Scenery (out of ten)
C: Eating out
D: Beaches
E: Total island appeal

Tourist Islands

	A	B	C	D	E
(1) **RHODES**: Best year-round climate. Quiet and lively spots.	***	8	10	9	9
(2) **PAROS**: Now developed for tourists with excellent sandy beaches.	***	8	10	9	9
(3) **CORFU**: Green and fertile with a gentle climate, but best to avoid July/August crowds.	****	10	10	9	8
(4) **SANTORINI**: Volcanic island with black beaches. Very popular with cruises.	****	8	10	9	8
(5) **MYKONOS**: Fashionable, cosmopolitan and touristy.	****	8	10	9	8

Quiet Islands

	A	B	C	D	E
(6) **PATMOS**: Unspoilt by tourism. Pretty harbour, good beaches.	**	8	8	6	9
(7) **KARPATHOS**: Just about to be 'discovered'. Mountainous, fertile, good beaches.	***	8	6	6	7
(8) **FOLEGANDROS**: Barren with beautiful main town. No packages but four ferries a week from Piraeus. Weekly ferry from Rhodes and Crete.	**	8	8	4	9
(9) **EFSTRATIOS**: Quiet and friendly. Difficult to find accommodation. No packages. Ferry from Evia and Kavala.	**	6	6	6	9
(10) **AMOULIANI**: Ideal for walking and swimming. Ferry from Tripita and Ouranoupolis. Accommodation in port. No packages.	*	6	4	3	9

Now read the article again carefully. If possible, work out the meaning of new words or, if you can't, look them up in a dictionary.

11. Reading comprehension

1 Which island is the most difficult to get to?
2 Which island has the most beautiful scenery, according to the guide?
3 Which island has the smallest number of restaurants to choose from?
4 Which island is the most crowded in the tourist season?
5 Which island could you go to at any time of the year, if you want good weather?
6 Which island will probably very soon become touristy?
7 On which island is it difficult to find anywhere to stay?
8 Why are the beaches on Santorini black?

12. Listening comprehension

Listen to the tape and write down which islands the people are on.

13. Writing

Write short descriptions of the main tourist areas, towns or cities in your country, like those in the newspaper article.

14. Discussion

1 If you could choose anywhere in the world for a holiday, where would you go?
2 'Every country should try to attract as many tourists as it can.' Do you agree?

Grammar summary

Is there There isn't	anybody anyone anything	in the room. (?)
There is	somebody someone something nobody no-one nothing	

I	like love enjoy hate don't mind dread can't stand	doing housework.

Let's	begin start go on stop	walking.

8

STEP ONE *The magician and the parrot*

The passengers on a Mediterranean cruise were entertained every night by a famous magician. And every night a parrot sat watching him. When the magician hid a rabbit in his pocket, the parrot cried, 'It's in his pocket! It's in his pocket!' When he hid a scarf up his sleeve, the parrot cried, 'It's up his sleeve! It's up his sleeve!'

It was the same every night. The magician stood there trying to entertain the passengers, and the parrot just sat there ruining all his tricks. The passengers loved it, but the magician didn't! When he heard the parrot giving away his secrets he was furious.

One evening, while the magician was showing the passengers a new and very difficult trick, there was a tremendous explosion. They felt the whole ship shaking. Two minutes later it was sinking. Just in time, the magician grabbed a lifejacket and jumped overboard.

After that he lay floating in the sea for many hours, until he saw an empty lifeboat. He climbed into it – exhausted.

He then lay sleeping in the back of the lifeboat until he heard a voice talking to him. He opened his eyes and saw the parrot staring at him from the other end of the boat.

After a time, the parrot slowly shook its head and said, 'OK, I give up. It's a good trick. Now tell me – where's the ship?'

1. Correct the sentences

Example: The passengers were on a Caribbean cruise.
No, they weren't. They were on a Mediterranean cruise.

1 They were entertained every night by a famous singer.

2 The magician used to hide a parrot in his pocket.

3 He also hid a rabbit up his sleeve.

4 The magician was pleased with the parrot.

5 Twelve minutes after the explosion, the ship was sinking.

6 Just in time, the parrot grabbed a lifejacket.

7 The magician lay floating in the sea for less than an hour.

8 He then lay sleeping in the front of the boat.

9 The parrot was in the back of the boat.

STEP TWO

2. Make true sentences

The magician stood there Every night a parrot sat The parrot just sat there The magician lay The parrot sat in the boat	floating in the sea. trying to entertain the passengers. staring at him. ruining his tricks. watching him.

He had to listen to The passengers felt He saw He heard	the whole ship a voice the parrot	talking to him. shaking. staring at him. giving away his secrets.

3. What did they do?

Use two verbs to describe what these people did.

Use: stand sit lie smell watch listen

burn watch sunbathe drink entertain shout

Example: *He lay sleeping.*

1

2

3

4

5

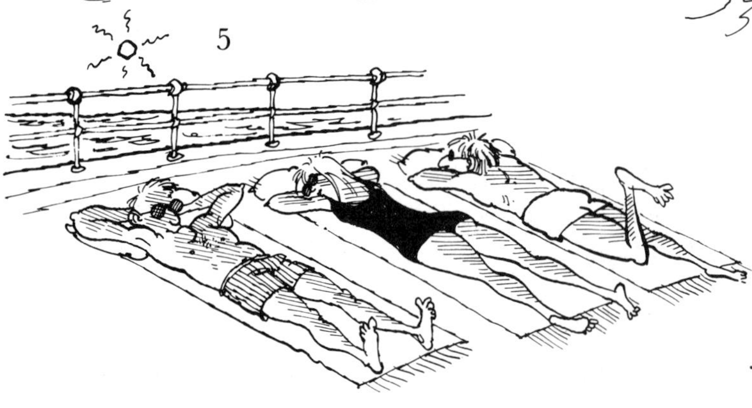

6

4. Beginning sentences

Begin the following sentences with one of these words or phrases:

After a time	Then
After that	Two minutes later
Just in time	When
Suddenly	While

__(1)__ the magician was entertaining the passengers, a parrot sat watching him. __(2)__ the parrot ruined his tricks, the magician was furious. __(3)__ there was a tremendous explosion. __(4)__ the ship sank. __(5)__ the magician jumped overboard. __(6)__ he lay floating in the sea for many hours. __(7)__ he lay down in the back of the boat. __(8)__ he heard a voice talking to him. __(9)__ he opened his eyes, he saw the parrot. __(10)__ the parrot spoke to him.

5. More talking animals

Put these sentences in the right order.

One of the elephants turned to the other.

They were looking through the menu when one of the horses called the waiter.

One day, two horses went into a restaurant and ordered a meal.

'Waiter', he said. 'This soup is cold.'

A few minutes later, two elephants came in and sat down at the next table.

'I don't believe it', he said. 'A talking horse!'

6. Telling jokes

Work with a friend. Tell him or her your favourite joke – in English!

STEP THREE *Killer bees*

Sharks, tarantula spiders and piranha fish have been used in horror movies. But bees? Surely not!

Wrong. There has been one already – and it was based on fact. Because killer bees exist. They just haven't reached the USA – yet.

It all started in 1957, in São Paulo, Brazil. A biologist was experimenting with two different kinds of bees, African and South American, to try and breed a bee which would make more honey.

The experiment failed. The bee that resulted was far more interested in making more bees than honey. And the bees were very aggressive and bad-tempered.

Then, by accident, 26 queen bees escaped. They started to breed immediately, and then spread everywhere. First through Brazil, and then up through Venezuela, Colombia and Central America. They spread at an average speed of about 650 kilometres a year, each colony producing four more colonies a year. This may not sound much, but in fact it means a million new colonies within five years.

Scientists have tried everything to stop them spreading – but so far nothing has worked.

But why is everybody in the southern states of the USA getting so scared? Because they've heard from the countries of South and Central America that these bees may *look* like ordinary bees, but in fact they are far more dangerous. Each bee can sting sixty times a minute, non-stop, for two hours, and between 400 and 500 stings are enough to kill a person. Hundreds of people in South America have already been killed. In the USA everyone now knows there's nothing they can do except wait . . .

7. An interview

Imagine an interview between an American living in the south of the USA and an expert on killer bees.

Ask the expert

1 where the killer bees come from originally.
2 how they are different from ordinary bees.

3 how fast they spread.
4 which countries they spread to after Brazil.
5 if anything was done to stop them spreading.
6 why they are dangerous.
7 how many people they have killed so far.

8. Complete the sentences

Put one of these words in the gaps in the following sentences.

each every everywhere everything everybody/everyone

1 Killer bees soon spread ______ in South America.
2 ______ was tried to stop them spreading but nothing worked.
3 There are now killer bees in ______ South American country.
4 ______ colony produces four more colonies a year.
5 ______ is scared of them.
6 ______ time you pick up a paper, you read about another person being killed by the bees.
7 ______ bee can sting sixty times a minute.
8 But not ______ who's been stung has died.
9 ______ in the USA knows they are coming.

9. In the news

Listen to the tape and then answer these questions.

1 Which country was Señor Gomez from?
2 How many times was he stung?
3 Where was he taken after the attack?
4 How many people have died from killer bee stings this year?

10. Work it out

1 How long ago were killer bees first bred?
2 How many kilometres do killer bees spread in two years?
3 How many colonies of killer bees can just one colony produce in two years?
4 How many times can a killer bee sting you in an hour?
5 How long would it take one bee to kill you if it stung you non-stop?

STEP FOUR ***Look it up***

This is a page from the Nelson ELT Pocket Dictionary. *Before you study it, look at these questions.*

1 What do the following letters (abbreviations) mean?
(a) ***n*** *(b)* ***v*** *(c)* ***adj*** *(d)* ***pt*** *(e)* ***pp*** *(f)* ***pl*** *(g)* ***coll*** *(h)* ***fig***

2 Which part tells you how to pronounce the words?

3 Why are some words in italics?

Now study the page. Look through it until you know the answers to the questions above. Answer them orally.

---

spade-work 255 **spectacular**

spade-work /ˈspeɪdwɜk/ *n (fig)* hard work needed in preparation for some undertaking
spaghetti /spəˈgetɪ/ *n (pl)* thin tubes of pasta
span /spæn/ *v pt* of **spin**
Spaniard /ˈspænɪəd/ *n* a native of Spain
Spanish /ˈspænɪʃ/ *adj* to do with Spain *n* the language of Spain
spank /spæŋk/ *v* to strike with the open hand on the buttocks, *usu* to punish a child *n* a blow with the open hand
spanking /ˈspæŋkɪŋ/ *adj* brisk *a spanking pace* *n* a slapping on the buttocks
spanner /ˈspænə(r)/ *n* a wrench, a tool for turning nuts on bolts, screws *etc*
throw a spanner in the works to sabotage a scheme
spare /speə(r)/ *v* **(sparing, spared) 1** to use in small quantities or to a small extent *Spare the rod and spoil the child.* **2** to do without *I can't spare the car today.* *adj* **1** extra, kept in reserve **2** thin, slender *a spare figure* **3** barely enough *a scanty allowance* *n* an extra part **sparing** *adj* **sparingly** *adv*
to spare above what is needed *time to spare*
spark /spɑk/ *n* **1** a tiny glowing particle thrown off by something burning **2** a small flash caused by an electric discharge
sparkle /ˈspɑkl/ *v* **(-ling, -led) 1** to give out flashes of light **2** *(fig)* to look bright *Her eyes sparkled.* **sparkling** *adj*
sparrow /ˈspærəʊ/ *n* a small brownish bird
sparse /spɑs/ *adj* **(-ser, -sest)** scanty
spasm /ˈspæzm/ *n* **1** a sudden jerk or tightening of a muscle that one cannot prevent **2** a violent but brief burst of activity or feeling *a spasm of energy, anger, fear*
spat /spæt/ *v pt* & *pp* of **spit**
spate /speɪt/ *n* **1** a strong flood, *esp* in a river **2** *(fig)* a sudden rush *a spate of orders*
speak /spik/ *v* **(-ing, spoke, spoken) 1** to utter words **2** to address an audience *The Prime Minister will speak on television tonight.* **3** to be able to use a language *Do you speak Italian?*
nothing to speak of nothing important
speak for oneself to express only one's personal opinion
speak out to express one's opinions clearly and boldly
speak up to speak loudly
speaker /ˈspikə(r)/ *n* **1** one who speaks **2** a loud-speaker **3** one who presides over an assembly such as the House of Commons
speaking /ˈspikɪŋ/ *adj* **1** concerned with uttering words *The play has only two speaking parts.* **2** vivid, striking *a speaking likeness*
on speaking terms 1 slightly acquainted with *She was on speaking terms with many eminent people.* **2** friendly *We are no longer on speaking terms with our neighbours.*
spear /spɪə(r)/ *n* a weapon consisting of a long shaft with a sharp, pointed head
spec /spek/ *n (coll)* speculation
on spec as a gamble *He bought the land on spec.*
special /ˈspeʃl/ *adj* **1** out of the ordinary *a special favour* **2** particular, not covered by a general rule *a special case* **specially** *adv*
specialist /ˈspeʃəlɪst/ *n* one who has expert knowledge or skill in a particular field, *esp* in medicine *a heart specialist*
specialize /ˈspeʃəlaɪz/ *v* **(-zing, -zed)** to become a specialist **specialization** *n*
species /ˈspiʃiz/ *n (pl* **species) 1** a division of a genus **2** a group of creatures or plants having common characteristics *the human species*
specific /spəˈsɪfɪk/ *adj* definite, precise *specific promises* **specifically** *adv*
specification /ˌspesɪfɪˈkeɪʃn/ *n* detailed information about something to be made or done
specify /ˈspesɪfaɪ/ *v* **(-fying, -fied)** to state definitely and in detail
specimen /ˈspesɪmən/ *n* **1** a sample, a person or thing regarded as representing a group **2** an item in a collection *specimens of Roman pottery* *adj* representative
speck /spek/ *n* a tiny spot or particle
spectacle /ˈspektəkl/ *n* **1** a sight, *esp* something striking *the spectacle of sunrise* **2** a public display **3** *(pl)* eyeglasses, lenses used to correct imperfect vision
see through rose-coloured spectacles to take a very optimistic view of things
spectacular /spekˈtækjʊlə(r)/ *adj* very impressive **spectacularly** *adv*

spade (mark on playing cards)

gardening spade

11. Reading comprehension

1 What is the connection between the words *spat* and *spit*?
2 Use the word *Spanish* in two examples, in two different ways.
3 Use these words in three different examples:
special specialist specialize
4 Put the following words in alphabetical order:
enjoyable engine enough enemy energetic enjoy English enormously engineering energy enormous engineer

12. Listening comprehension

Listen to the definitions of words on the tape and write down what the words are.

13. Writing

Write definitions of the following words, and include an example of how to use each word.

Example: beat – *to hit a number of times*
The man beat the horse with a stick.

(1) battery (2) beach (3) bear (4) beard (5) beautiful
(6) bed (7) bee (8) before (9) begin (10) behind

14. Discussion

1 'Learning English is easy. All you have to do is learn what a number of English words mean in your own language.' Do you agree?
2 Do you think children learn languages more easily than adults?

Grammar summary

<table>
<tr><td>He</td><td>sat
lay
stood</td><td>waiting.</td></tr>
</table>

<table>
<tr><td>Each
Every</td><td>person</td><td rowspan="2">wants something different.</td></tr>
<tr><td colspan="2">Everyone
Everybody</td></tr>
</table>

<table>
<tr><td rowspan="2">I</td><td>can</td><td>see
hear
feel
smell</td><td rowspan="2">something</td><td rowspan="2">burning.</td></tr>
<tr><td colspan="2">watched
listened to</td></tr>
</table>

9

STEP ONE *The face at the window*

My cousin Alexander was, like me, an only child. So when we were not at school, we often used to stay with each other. We were more like brothers than cousins.

My uncle Charles, Alexander's father, was a professor of biology at Oxford University. He did brilliant, original research, or so my parents said. I asked him once what sort of research it was. He muttered something about 'the mutation of species' and 'biological engineering'. I couldn't understand him, and he obviously didn't want to explain, so I didn't ask him again. Alexander told me that he'd visited his father's laboratories at the university, and he'd been surprised to see, in addition to the usual rats and rabbits you'd expect to see in a biology laboratory, a young gorilla.

Then, suddenly, Alexander's father lost his job. I wasn't told why they had sacked him, and my parents never talked about it, at least not in front of me. That was at the beginning of the summer. At the end of the summer it was my turn to go and stay with Alexander.

I was surprised when he didn't meet me at the station, as we'd arranged. But it wasn't a long walk to his home. I knocked at the front door. After I'd waited for more than a minute my aunt came to the door. Instead of welcoming me, she just stood there, wringing her hands.

'Oh, it's you, Richard,' she said, finally.
'Of course it's me. I've come to stay, remember?'
'Oh, dear, didn't you get my letter?'
'No. What letter?'
'It was about your cousin Alexander. You see, he's had an accident, a terrible accident.'
'Oh, no! What sort of accident? Is he in hospital?'
'Well, no, not exactly. It's just that something went wrong, horribly wrong, and . . .'

Just then I caught sight of a face looking down at me from an upstairs window. 'I don't believe it!' I blurted out.

It was a weird face, half man, half ape. But its eyes were what I noticed most. Beneath the low, sloping forehead and jutting eyebrows of a gorilla I could see that the eyes were unmistakably those of my cousin Alexander.

1. Ask Richard

Work in pairs. One of you is Richard. Ask him

1 if he's got any brothers or sisters.
2 if he went to the same school as Alexander.
3 what his uncle Charles's job was.
4 what his uncle Charles did research into.
5 when his uncle lost his job.
6 when he went to visit Alexander.
7 how he got to Alexander's house.
8 who came to the door.
9 why she was surprised to see him.
10 what had happened to Alexander.
11 what he saw at an upstairs window.

STEP TWO

2. What happened then?

Describe in a few lines what happened after he saw the face at the window.

3. Make true sentences

Alexander's mother Alexander's father Alexander Richard	had	visited his father's laboratory. lost his job. walked from the station. sent Richard a letter. asked his uncle about his research. made a terrible mistake. been a professor of biology. stayed with Alexander before.

4. The definite article

Put 'the' in the gaps in the following, if necessary.

'I'm sixteen and I'm still at ___(1)___ school. ___(2)___ school I go to is not far from where I live. I probably won't leave ___(3)___ school until I'm eighteen. After I leave ___(4)___ school I'll probably go to ___(5)___ university – at least that's what my parents want me to do. Normally it's quite easy to get into ___(6)___ university. But ___(7)___ university I want to go to is very difficult to get into.'

'My father's in ___(8)___ hospital at the moment. They sent him to ___(9)___ hospital to have an operation. My mother and me visit him in ___(10)___ hospital every day although ___(11)___ hospital is nearly twenty kilometres away. I hate ___(12)___ hospitals, particularly ___(13)___ hospital he's in. I think it must be the smell.'

5. Finish the sentences

Think of your own way of completing these sentences.

1 Alexander's father lost his job because . . .
2 There was a young gorilla in his laboratory because . . .
3 Nobody met him at the station because . . .
4 Alexander's mother wrung her hands because . . .
5 The face at the window had Alexander's eyes because . . .

Compare your sentences with other students'.

6. Ask a friend

Ask him/her

1 if he/she is an only child.
2 how many cousins he/she has got.
3 if he/she ever goes to stay with any of his/her cousins.
4 how many uncles or aunts he/she has got.
5 if he/she studies biology.
6 how much he/she knows about biological engineering.
7 if he/she has ever been in a biology laboratory. (What animals were there in there?)
8 if he/she has ever been to hospital.
9 if he/she has ever seen a gorilla.

STEP THREE *Odd facts about hair*

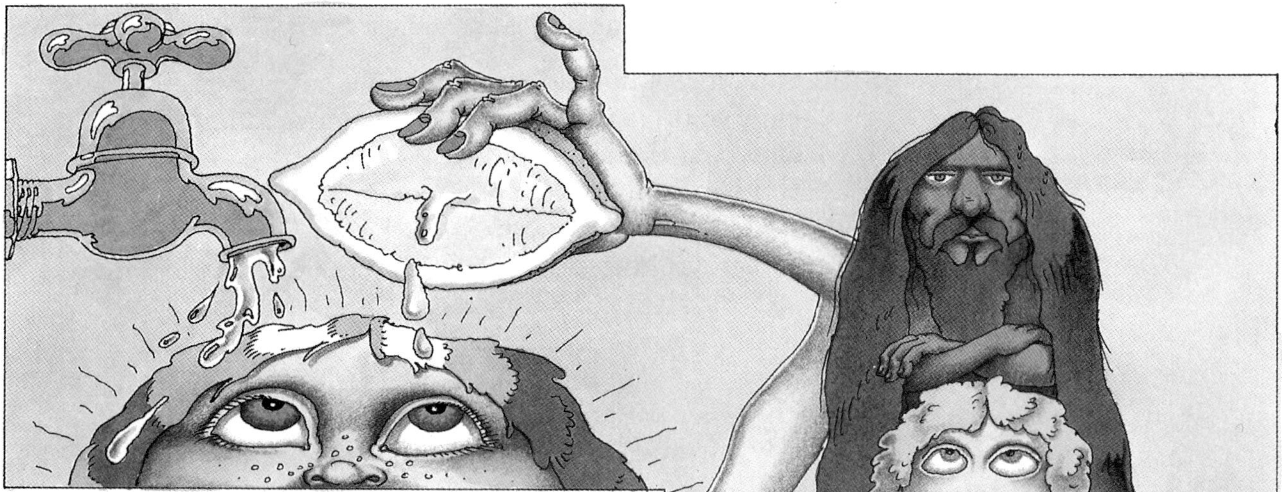

Most people have about 20,000 hairs on their head. Each hair grows about one centimetre a month, and although it's dead from the root up, it can stay on your head for several years, after which it falls out naturally. The speed at which your hair grows does not change according to how often you cut it.

Most people lose between 50 and 100 hairs a day. If you are very worried about something, you will probably lose a great many more.

If you want healthy hair, eat plenty of vitamins A, B and D.

A lot of people use expensive conditioners to make their hair look shiny. They could save themselves quite a lot of money if they used lemon juice and cold water instead.

The word 'shampoo' comes from a Hindi word meaning 'to press'.

Blondes have the most hair, and redheads have the least (but also the thickest).

The person with the longest hair in the world was an Indian, Swami Pandarasannadhi. His hair was just over 7.93 metres long.

7. Questions and answers

Pair off questions and answers.

1 How many hairs do most people have on their heads?
2 How many hairs do most people lose a day?
3 How fast does hair grow?
4 How can you make your hair look shiny?
5 Which people have the most hair?
6 Which vitamin do dairy products particularly contain?

(a) Between 50 and 100.
(b) By washing it in cold water.
(c) D.
(d) Those with blonde hair.
(e) About 20,000.
(f) About one centimetre a month.

8. Write true sentences

Most Several (Quite) a lot of A great many	people	in this class in this school in this area/town in this country	. . .

Compare your sentences with other students'.

9. Ask a friend

Ask

1 how often he/she washes his/her hair.
2 if he/she uses a shampoo. (What kind of shampoo?)
3 if he/she uses a conditioner. (Is it expensive?)
4 how he/she dries his/her hair.
5 if he/she would like it to be straighter or more curly.
6 if he/she would like it to be a different colour.
7 how often he/she cuts it.
8 who cuts it.

10. An advertisement

Write an advertisement for an expensive conditioner in which it is claimed that your hair will look healthier, more shiny, etc., if you use it. Work in groups if you like.

11. How much money?

Listen to the tape. Then answer these two questions.

1 How much money did she spend?
2 How much money did she come home with?

12. Which is right?

1 The most / Most / The most many — people have black hair.

2 You must eat — plenty of / plenty / a plenty of — vitamins if you want healthy hair.

3 There are — lot of / a lot / a lot of — vitamins in dairy products.

4 You lose — a quite lot of / quite a lot of / quite a lot — hairs every day.

5 Conditioners are — the most expensive / the expensivest / most expensive — way of making your hair look shiny.

6 Several / Several of / The several — people in our family have red hair.

7 Redheads have — the less / the least / the most little — number of hairs on their heads.

8 A great many / Great many / Great a many — people never wash their hair with shampoo.

STEP FOUR ***Breaking up***

This is a passage from the novel Sons and Lovers *by the English writer D. H. Lawrence. Before you read it, look at these questions.*
1 What does Paul try to tell Miriam?
2 Why doesn't Miriam understand him?
3 Does she want to break off the relationship too?
Now read the passage. At the end of it you should be able to discuss the questions above. Compare your answers orally.

(Paul, the main character in the book, has been going out with Miriam, a farmer's daughter, for some time. He has now decided that he wants to end the relationship – but he is finding it difficult to do so.)

'Why are you sad?' she asked humbly.

'I'm not sad; why should I be?' he answered. 'I'm only normal.'

She wondered why he always claimed to be normal when he was disagreeable.

'But what is the matter?' she pleaded.

'Nothing!'

'Nay!' she murmured.

He picked up a stick and began to stab the earth with it.

'You'd far better not talk,' he said.

'But I wish to know –' she replied.

He laughed.

'You always do,' he said.

'It's not fair to me,' she murmured.

He thrust, thrust, thrust at the ground with the pointed stick. She gently and firmly laid her hand on his wrist.

'Don't!' she said. 'Put it away.'

He flung the stick into the bushes, and leaned back. Now he was bottled up.

'What is it?' she pleaded softly.

He lay perfectly still, only his eyes alive, and they full of torment.

'You know,' he said at length, rather wearily – 'you know – we'd better break off.'

It was what she dreaded. Everything seemed to darken before her eyes.

'Why?' she murmured. 'What has happened?'

'Nothing has happened. We only realise where we are. It's no good –'

She waited in silence, sadly, patiently. It was no good being impatient with him. At any rate, he would tell her now what troubled him.

'We agreed on friendship,' he went on in a dull, monotonous voice. 'How often *have* we agreed for friendship! And yet – it neither stops there, nor gets anywhere else.'

He was silent again. She brooded. What did he mean? He was so wearying. There was something he would not say. Yet she must be patient with him.

Now read the passage again carefully. If possible, work out the meaning of new words or, if you can't, look them up in a dictionary.

13. Reading comprehension

1 Who do you think the following adjectives best describe – Paul or Miriam?

disagreeable patient tense humble
irritated gentle sad tormented

2 What sort of people are Paul and Miriam?
3 What are the main differences between them?
4 What does Paul do to show he is tense?
5 Why do *you* think Paul wants to break off the relationship?

14. Listening comprehension

Listen to the tape and decide whether Paul or Miriam would say these things.

15. Writing

Continue the conversation between Paul and Miriam in any way you like.

16. Discussion

1 If you had a boyfriend/girlfriend, how would you end the relationship?
2 'Just because a relationship has ended, it doesn't mean that the two people can't still be friends.' Do you agree?

Grammar summary

He's	at in	university. school. hospital.
He works	at a in a	

Blondes Redheads	have	the most the least	hair.

10

STEP ONE

Across Australia - for free!

Sometime in the not-too-distant future the world's oil reserves are going to run out. But people are probably still going to want to travel in their own cars. So what kind of fuel are they going to use? There are, already, cars powered by electricity and by gas. But how about a car powered by sunlight? One which can drive from one side of Australia to the other – a distance of over 4,000 kilometres – without refuelling once. In other words, for free.

It's not the kind of car you can just go out and buy. Not yet, anyway. In fact there's only one car like it. It's called the Quiet Achiever. By driving from Perth on the west coast of Australia to Sydney on the east coast it proved that a car powered by sunlight is a practical and extremely economical possibility.

The Quiet Achiever is the invention of a 32-year-old racing driver, Larry Perkins. It looks a bit like a giant bath on bicycle wheels, with a table tennis table for a roof. In fact, the roof is covered with solar panels and these feed two 12-volt car batteries which power a small 1-horsepower, 24-volt electric motor driving the back wheels.

It isn't a particularly fast car. Its maximum speed is only about 60 kph, and that's downhill with the wind behind. Its only controls are an ammeter, a speedometer and brakes from a bicycle, which work only on the back wheels.

On his arrival in Sydney, Larry Perkins told reporters, 'It was quite comfortable, really. While I was driving along, I had some cassettes to listen to, and even without windows it didn't get too hot because I was always in the shade. While the sun was shining we were all right. So, during the day, I could drive more or less non-stop from sunrise to sunset. But as soon as the sun went behind a cloud I noticed the amps dropped. During the winter, or in countries like Britain, I suppose you'd just have to put it in your garage and wait for the sun to come out!'

1. Questions and answers

Pair off questions and answers in the two columns. Work with a partner.

1 Where did Larry Perkins start his journey from?
2 What's the maximum speed of the Quiet Achiever?
3 Where did he drive to?
4 How far is it from Perth to Sydney?
5 How old was Larry Perkins?
6 How many batteries did the car have?
7 How powerful was the electric motor?
8 How many times did it stop to refuel?

(a) 60 kph
(b) Sydney
(c) 32
(d) 2
(e) Perth
(f) Over 4,000 kilometres
(g) None
(h) One horsepower

STEP TWO

2. Make sentences

During While	the sun was shining the journey the winter the day he was driving	he listened to cassettes. he never stopped to refuel. he drove from sunrise to sunset. the amps didn't drop. you couldn't use a solar-powered car.

3. Measures

Make sentences.

You measure	distance weight height temperature speed power electric current electric potential	in	horsepower. degrees. kilometres. kilometres per hour. kilos. metres. volts. amperes (amps).

4. Word building

Complete the following sentences using words related to those in brackets.

Example: Cars powered by ______ are not new. (electric)
Cars powered by *electricity* are not new.

1 The ______ from Perth to Sydney is over 4,000 kilometres. (distant)

2 The Quiet Achiever is not a ______ fast car. (particular)

3 But it crossed Australia without ______ once. (fuel)

4 It is the ______ of an Australian called Larry Perkins. (invent)

5 ______ is at 5.15 a.m. tomorrow and ______ is at 8.43 p.m. (sun)

6 It is ______ to use solar-powered cars in cold countries. (possible)

7 Larry Perkins proved his point by ______ across Australia. (drive)

8 His ______ was greeted by headlines in all the Australian newspapers. (arrive)

5. Discussion

If you were a car manufacturer, would you try to develop Larry Perkins' idea? (Why/Why not?)

Discuss your ideas and reasons in groups.

STEP THREE — *Would you believe it?*

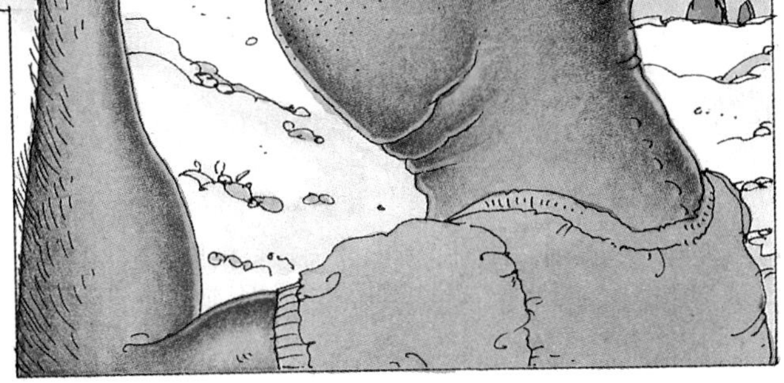

Wrong way round

The landlord of a pub in Nottingham, Mr John Weller, was surprised by the fact that all 24 photographs which he'd taken on his holiday in Greece were of his right ear. He was unable to understand why until it was explained to him that he had held his new camera the wrong way round.

Unhappy ending

A Los Angeles couple were sent two tickets to a play they wanted to see. But they were not able to thank the person they were sent by. There was only a note with the tickets which said, 'Guess who?'

They went to the play and enjoyed it very much. But when they got home, they found that a window at the back of the house was broken. Inside, the contents of their drawers were scattered everywhere. All their valuables were stolen.

There was a note on the kitchen table. It said, 'Now you know!'

Sorry, can't stop

The buses between the towns of Bradford-on-Avon and Trowbridge were often late and sometimes never came at all. Mr Harold Parkinson, the new manager of the bus company, was told to improve the service. Mr Parkinson worked hard. In less than a month, a new timetable was introduced.

Mr Parkinson was disappointed by the number of people who complained to him during the first week. They said buses often drove straight past long queues of people waiting at the bus stops.

Mr Parkinson replied, 'If these buses stopped to pick up passengers, we would not be able to keep to the new timetable.'

6. Make sentences

Mr Weller It A Los Angeles couple They couldn't thank the people the tickets The contents of their drawers All their valuables Mr Parkinson A new timetable	was were	sent tickets to a play. explained to him that he'd held his camera the wrong way. surprised by his Greek holiday photographs. scattered everywhere. sent by. soon introduced. told to improve the bus service. stolen.

7. Interviews

Ask Mr Weller

1 what his job is.
2 where he went for his holiday.
3 why he was surprised by his photographs.
4 what his mistake was.

Ask the Los Angeles couple

1 what they were sent.
2 why they couldn't thank the sender.
3 when they first realised something was wrong.
4 what was on the kitchen table.

Ask Mr Parkinson

1 why he was told to improve the bus service.
2 how long it took him to write a new timetable.
3 why he was disappointed.
4 what would happen if the buses stopped to pick up passengers.

Act out your interviews in pairs.

8. Dialogues

Write short dialogues for one of these situations. Work in pairs and then act out your dialogues.

1 Mr Weller shows his Greek holiday photograph to a friend, and the friend explains why they are all of his right ear.
2 The Los Angeles couple have just read the note which said, 'Now you know!'
3 An angry passenger complains about the bus service to Mr Parkinson.

9. Listening

Listen to the tape and mark these words in the order you hear them (1, 2 or 3).

1 he'd hid hide
2 were war worse
3 wide white wait
4 ear air hear
5 way why we
6 see say seem
7 P be V
8 said sad side
9 went want won't
10 house whose horse
11 town torn ton
12 late let light

10. Change the sentences

Change these sentences from active to passive. The main verb is the word in italics.

Example: 'My wife *gave* me a new camera for my birthday.'
'I was given a new camera for my birthday.'

1 'My friends *told* me what I had done wrong.'
2 'Somebody *stole* our TV while we were at the theatre.'
3 'The thieves *stuck* a note to the kitchen table.'
4 'The buses *left* us standing at the bus stops.'
5 'People *asked* me to change the timetable.'

STEP FOUR *Caring for the countryside*

This is a series of rules or guidelines published by the Australian Ministry of the Environment. Before you read them, look at these questions.

1 Can you name one thing which there is a particular danger of in Australia?

2 Can you name one thing which there is a shortage of in Australia?

3 What else do you learn from the rules which is particular or unique to Australia?

Now read the rules. By the end you should know the answers to the three questions above. Answer them orally.

A Countryside Code for Australia

1 Gates on properties should be left as they are found, open or closed.
2 Other people's property should be respected – fences should not be cut, broken or stretched by climbing over them.
3 "Souveniring" is another name for stealing. Nothing should be removed from a property without the owner's permission.
4 Dogs or cats should never be abandoned in the bush – they will kill and eat wildlife to survive. Dogs must never be allowed to disturb stock.
5 Vehicles should be driven slowly over dusty roads and when approaching stock.
6 Live matches or cigarettes should not be thrown from moving or stationary vehicles.
7 Fire can kill – extreme care must be taken when lighting fires, and they must be extinguished. Be aware of fire bans before lighting fires.
8 Streams should not be used as toilets.
9 Names and initials should not be placed on natural features or Aboriginal carvings – these are part of the national estate.
10 Clean water is scarce – salt or fresh, it should not be polluted with soap, detergents or litter.
11 Proper precautions should be taken before bushwalking or driving into rough country. Lives can be lost in rescue operations.
12 A licence is necessary if you want to search for gold or gems. Holes must be filled in.

Read the rules again. If possible, work out the meaning of new words or, if you can't, look them up in a dictionary.

11. Reading comprehension

Now decide if the following statements are true or false.

1 Gates should be left closed.
2 Fences are often broken or stretched.
3 'Stealing' is another word for 'souveniring'.
4 Cats and dogs cannot survive in the bush.
5 Drivers should only throw cigarettes out of vehicles which are not moving.
6 Don't light a fire if there is a fire ban.
7 Aboriginals often carve their initials on natural features.
8 Soap and detergents only pollute fresh water.
9 People sometimes die when trying to rescue bushwalkers.
10 People who find gold or gems must then get a licence.

12. Listening comprehension

Listen to the tape and write down the number of the rule which some people are breaking.

13. Writing

Write a short extract from a Countryside Code in which you concentrate on rules which are special for your country.

14. Discussion

1 'The only people who understand the countryside are the people who live and work in it; others only cause damage.' Do you agree?
2 Do you think 'wild' countryside should be preserved?

Grammar summary

<table>
<tr><td rowspan="2">They drove</td><td>during</td><td>the day.</td></tr>
<tr><td>while</td><td>the sun was shining.</td></tr>
</table>

<table>
<tr><td>I
He
She</td><td>was</td><td rowspan="2">sent tickets.</td></tr>
<tr><td>You
We
They</td><td>were</td></tr>
</table>

Three hundred voices shout together:

> We're heading for success,
> We're passing all the rest,
> S – U – C – C – E – S – S,
> We are the best!

Then three hundred extremely energetic girls, all between fifteen and seventeen, jump high into the air, their arms and legs spread as wide as they'll go.

These are cheerleaders – the most popular, the most attractive and the most admired teenagers in the USA, or so they hope. They're at a special summer camp for cheerleaders, where in one short week they are taught dozens of new jumps and stunts. It's certainly the most tiring holiday they'll ever have. After 13 hours in 37° heat their instructor, Delia Katz, yells at them, 'Are you tired?' 'No!' they yell back. 'Are you hot or hungry?' 'No!' they shout at her, the sweat pouring off them. 'Are you still full of go?' 'Yeah!' they scream, kicking and jumping high in the air just to prove it.

There are over half a million cheerleaders in the USA, and nearly half of them are sent to these special summer camps, or 'clinics' as they are called.

Delia Katz, who modestly describes her clinic as 'the best in the west', has been cheerleading since she was only six. 'Every girl wants to be a cheerleader. If you are chosen for a High School's cheerleaders' squad, it's the greatest moment in your life – it's to be in heaven. It means you're really *special*! Parents come to me, before their daughters even start at High School, and ask me the best way to help them get into the squad. I haven't actually been offered money by any of them yet, but the worst of them have come pretty close!'

Only one girl is chosen from the fifty who try for each place in the squad. And each of these fifty must first be recommended by her class teacher.

But the really hard work starts after they've been lucky enough to be selected. Cheerleaders have to practise for two hours a day after school. They must diet, if necessary, to make sure they're always 50 kilos (if they're the ideal 1 metre 70 tall). They must be healthy, and above all they must be taught to *smile* all the time – because cheerleaders must always look cheerful, enthusiastic and happy.

Lorraine Oligino, 16, was asked the simple question, 'Why are you a cheerleader?'

'That's a pretty dumb question! Because I just love it – I love being watched, being the center of attention, I mean. When I'm out there with the players, performing and leading the crowd, I know they're all looking at me and thinking, "Wow, she's good-looking!" or "I just wish *I* could do that!" You see, we're different. At school, we're allowed to wear special cheerleaders' jackets with our name on the back. And we go to games on the same bus as the players. So, naturally, we're dated by them. What a difference for our status – and theirs!'

It is the end of a long, tiring day and the 300 girls are being given a final pep talk by Delia Katz. 'This is the most exciting time of your lives. It's all happening to you, right now. So make the most of it, don't waste a moment, enjoy it. Live the Dream. And remember, girls, *smile!*'

1. Interview Lorraine Oligino

Work in pairs. One of you is Lorraine. Complete the questions first.

Example: What/name?
– *What's your name?*
– *Lorraine Oligino.*

1 How old/you?

2 Why/cheerleader?

3 What/enjoy most?

4 How/cheerleader?

5 How long/this clinic?

6 What/ideal weight/cheerleader?

7 What/ideal height?

8 Why/smile all the time?

9 Tired?

STEP TWO

2. Change the sentences

Change the following sentences from active to passive.

Example: Most High School students admire cheerleaders.
Cheerleaders are admired by most High School students.

1 Delia Katz is teaching the girls some new stunts.
2 Basketball players often date cheerleaders.
3 Class teachers recommend cheerleaders.
4 Parents have never offered Delia Katz money.
5 Delia Katz is giving them a final pep talk.

3. Who?

Change the following sentences from passive to active. To start your sentences, choose from:

schools	the writer	Delia Katz

Example: The girls are given no time to rest.
Delia Katz gives the girls no time to rest.

1 They are told to smile the whole time.
2 Over 200,000 cheerleaders are sent to special summer camps.
3 Lorraine Oligino was asked, 'Why are you a cheerleader?'
4 The special summer camps are called 'clinics'.
5 Cheerleaders are allowed to wear special jackets.

4. A description

Make a list of the words in the text which you can use to describe people. Write down, where possible, their opposites.

Now describe a person in your class or a person in your family using as many of the words from your list as possible.

5. Write sentences

Example: energetic person
The most energetic person I know is my 70-year-old grandfather.

1 cheerful person
2 attractive person
3 good-looking person
4 popular people
5 modest person
6 great moment/my life
7 bad moment/my life
8 tiring holiday
9 good holiday
10 exciting time

Now ask the person sitting next to you questions like:

Who's the most cheerful person you know?

6. Which would you rather be?

Arrange these adjectives in order of preference.

popular
admired
happy
good-looking
healthy
successful

Now think of other adjectives that you would like to hear said about you. Compare your list with others and discuss in what way they are different.

7. An advertisement

Write an advertisement for Delia Katz's 'clinic' for cheerleaders, including as much information from the text as you can. Work in groups.

8. Listen and complete

Dear Mom,
I'm having a great time!
I've been here for only (1____)
days but already I've learnt
(2____) new (3____) and (4____) new
(5____). There are (6____) girls
here at the (7____). All of us
are between (8____) and (9____).
We've been working so hard -
for (10____) hours a day, with
temperature at (11____) -
that I've already lost (12____)
kilos.
See you on (13____)
love, Lorraine

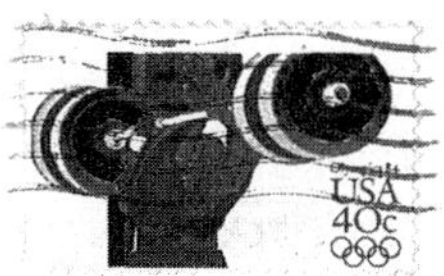

Mrs J. Oligino
2401 South St.
Boston
Mass 01867

STEP THREE *The schoolboy businessman*

Tony Burton is only 17 and still at school, but he already has his own company.

– What sort of company do you have?

– It's a computer company.

– You mean you make your own computers?

– No, I leave that to the big companies. I just design the software.

– What is software, exactly?

– That's the word we have for all sorts of computer programs.

– How many employees does your company have?

– Only one, actually, and that's myself.

– When did you first get interested in computers?

– When I was about ten, I suppose. My uncle's company had a computer, and he used to let me have a go with it after everybody else had gone home. Soon I was spending every spare minute I had on it. My friends were all off having a good time playing football or talking to girls. I was always at my computer. My mother complained, I remember, because often I didn't even have meals.

– Did you teach yourself to operate it, or did you have lessons?

– One of the programmers taught me.

– So now you're a programmer yourself?

– Yes, but I also help companies who want to computerise.

– Do you have any difficulties going to school and being a businessman at the same time?

– It's a bit difficult but my mother answers the phone while I'm at school – people think she's my secretary. Then, if it's something urgent, she 'bleeps' me. I have this bleeper here in my pocket, and I leave school as soon as possible.

– In your school uniform?

– No, that would ruin my reputation as a businessman. I keep a suit in my school bag for a quick change of image!

9. Interview Mrs Burton

Ask her about Tony, his company, how it started and how she helps him. Use phrases like:

What sort of . . .?
You mean . . .?
. . . exactly?
When did . . .?
Did you . . .?
So . . .?

10. Fill the gaps

Use: has (doesn't) have had didn't have are having

His company ___(1)___ only one employee. It ___(2)___ a secretary.
– Do you ___(3)___ a bleeper?
– Yes, I ___(4)___ one in my pocket.
Tony also ___(5)___ a suit in his school bag. He ___(6)___ any customers when he started.
Now he ___(7)___ over twenty.
– Did you ___(8)___ a holiday last year?
– No, I ___(9)___ enough time. I ___(10)___ too much work to do.
– What are your friends doing?
– They ___(11)___ good time, I suppose. They ___(12)___ girlfriends, but I ___(13)___ a computer!

11. Role play

Work in pairs. One of you is Tony's mother.

Client	Tony's mother
Ask to speak to Tony Burton.	Tell him/her Tony is not there.
Ask who you are speaking to.	Tell him/her you are Mr Burton's secretary. Ask if it is urgent.
Tell her it is urgent.	Offer to contact Mr Burton. Ask where to reach the caller.
Give your name and telephone number.	Repeat the information. Say goodbye.
Respond.	

STEP FOUR *Brain box*

This is an article from Which?, *a British consumers' magazine. Before you read it, look at these questions.*

1 Would a home computer be of more benefit to parents or to their children?

2 What are the best reasons for buying a home computer?

3 What are the main reasons why a home computer is not really very useful, according to the article?

Now read the article. By the end of it you should know the answers to the three questions above. Answer them orally.

WHAT HOME COMPUTERS CAN AND CAN'T DO

CAN THEY HELP YOU LEARN ABOUT COMPUTERS?
YES: just about any computer will give you some understanding – you could pay less than £100.

CAN THEY PLAY GAMES?
YES: easily the most popular use. A computer set up to play games can cost around £150. Each game costs around £5 to £40. If you just want to play games, an electronic games machine is cheaper.

CAN THEY MAKE MUSIC?
MAYBE: many can manage simple tunes – cost about £200 upwards. But you'd have to spend a lot more to compete with a music synthesiser.

CAN THEY DRAW PICTURES?
DEPENDS: all can manage some sort of drawings, but for colourful creations with smooth curves and lots of detail, you'll need to pay around £300 to £400 – plus, perhaps, £250 for a display unit to see the pictures to their best advantage.

CAN THEY EDUCATE YOUR KIDS?
YES: a top reason for getting a computer. But how much you'll need to spend depends on what subject they want to learn and whether you want the same system as your school has – which can make a lot of sense.

CAN THEY KEEP YOUR FINANCES STRAIGHT?
POSSIBLE: can be done on the cheap for less than £200. A calculator and pen and paper will be cheaper still and probably more convenient.

CAN THEY CHART THE CONTENTS OF YOUR FREEZER AND PLAN MEALS FOR THE MONTH AHEAD?
NO: you'd spend so long keeping the computer updated with what you had used, you wouldn't have much time left for eating.

CAN THEY CONTROL THE CENTRAL HEATING?
NO: some could, but if you knew enough to make them do it, you should know enough to realise it's more cost-effective to stick to straightforward time clocks or thermostats.

CAN THEY KEEP THE NAMES AND ADDRESSES OF THE MEMBERS OF YOUR GARDENING CLUB?
MAYBE: it depends how many members and what you want the addresses for — for more than a few hundred names you could find yourself spending £1000 to make it worthwhile.

CAN THEY GIVE YOU A TYPEWRITER WITH A MEMORY?
POSSIBLE: but apart from the very simplest jobs, you need so many extras it's no longer a cheap home computer.

CAN THEY MAKE YOUR FORTUNE?
NO: more likely to make your child's. There's not a lot of money to be made writing and selling programs (the computer's instructions) unless you are both good and prolific. So much of the money that is made goes to teenagers who seem to be both.

Read the article again. If possible, work out the meaning of new words or, if you can't, look them up in a dictionary.

12. Reading comprehension

1 Why is it cheaper to buy an electronic games machine than a computer if you only want to play games?
2 Do you have to have a display unit if you want to draw pictures with your computer?
3 Why is a calculator, pen and paper better than a computer at keeping your finances straight?
4 Why is it not a good idea to computerise the contents of your freezer?
5 What is the most cost-effective way of controlling your central heating?

13. Listening comprehension

Listen to the tape and decide which of the statements are true and which are false.

14. Writing

Write a short list, similar to the one in the article, of what one of the following machines can or can't do.

a pocket calculator
a cassette recorder
a digital watch with many functions

15. Discussion

1 'Knowing how to use a computer will soon be as important as knowing how to read and write.' Do you agree?
2 How do you think computers will change our lives in the next twenty years?

Grammar summary

I	am	
He She It	is	admired.
We You They	are	

I	am		
He She It	is	being	taught.
We You They	are		

I We You They	have	been	chosen.
He She It	has		

Boatloads of poor immigrants arriving in the 'promised land' of the United States at the end of the last century were first greeted by a bronze and iron lady – the Statue of Liberty.

The statue is on Liberty Island, fifteen minutes by sightseeing ferry from Manhattan. It was the work of a French sculptor, and it was a gift from the French people to the people of the United States. As the sculptor finished the various parts of the body, they were shown all over France, and people gave money which helped to pay for the next part of the body.

Then, in 1884, all the parts were put together for the first time in Paris to make sure they were the right size. They were, so the whole statue, which weighed over 200 tonnes, was taken to pieces again, put into crates and sent across the Atlantic to America.

There, in 1886, it was erected, and for the next thirteen years it was the tallest structure on that side of the Atlantic. The lady's head was over 100 metres above the ground. Today, however, it is only as tall as an ordinary New York department store.

Nowadays, the Statue of Liberty attracts ferryloads of tourists instead of boatloads of immigrants. They take trips around Liberty

Island, or they land and squeeze into the elevator which takes them as far as the lady's left shoulder. They then have to climb 160 steps to the top of her head. On their way they can recognise, from the inside, different parts of her face – like her chin, her mouth and her nose. Her nose alone is over three metres wide. From the outside, some people say, she looks a bit like the young Marlon Brando.

From the crown on the top of her head tourists can then look out towards the famous skyline of Manhattan. It is possible to climb up her right arm to the torch she is holding in her hand. But it is only a tunnel with narrow winding stairs, with no room for people to squeeze past each other. So ordinary tourists are not allowed up because there could be 'jams' if somebody got half-way up and then changed his mind!

1. What is the question?

Complete the questions and then answer them. Work in pairs.

Example: Where . . . made?
France
– *Where was the Statue of Liberty made?*
– *It was made in France.*

1 What . . . made of?
bronze and iron

2 Where . . . ?
on Liberty Island

3 How far . . . Manhattan?
15 minutes by sightseeing ferry

4 Where . . . from?
from France

5 When . . . erected?
in 1886

6 How far . . . ground?
over 100 metres

7 How many . . . head?
160

8 How . . . mouth?
over three metres

9 What . . . head?
the skyline of Manhattan

10 What . . . hand?
a torch

STEP TWO

2. Where are they?

Complete the sentences.

1 The statue is ______ an island, ______ its tip.

2 The island is ______ the entrance ______ New York Harbour.

3 It is three kilometres ______ the tip ______ Manhattan ______ Liberty Island.

4 The torch is ______ her hand, ______ her head.

5 The crown is ______ her head.

6 The head is 100 metres ______ the ground.

7 From ______ the statue you can see the different parts ______ her face.

8 From the ______ she looks a bit like Marlon Brando.

3. Movement

Make the following sentences complete. Use:

around into off onto out of past towards under

1 First the boat went ______ the harbour.

2 Then it went ______ the island.

3 Then it went ______ the lighthouse.

4 It went ______ the bridge ______ the dock.

5 After that it went ______ the harbour again.

6 There the passengers got ______ the boat and ______ dry land.

4. A return gift

What do you think would be a suitable return gift from the people of the United States to the people of France to mark the statue's centenary? Discuss your ideas in groups.

5. A guided tour of New York

Listen to the tape and follow the route on the map.

1 Which street did they go along from Times Square?
2 What's the name of the railway station they passed?
3 What's the name of the river they had on their right-hand side?
4 What building was completed in 1952?
5 What's the name of the bridge?
6 Which island does the bridge lead to?
7 Which avenue were they driving down?
8 What's the name of the famous building they passed?
9 What's the name of the artistic area of New York?
10 What's the name of the huge, 110-storey high building?
11 What could they see looking out over the Hudson River?

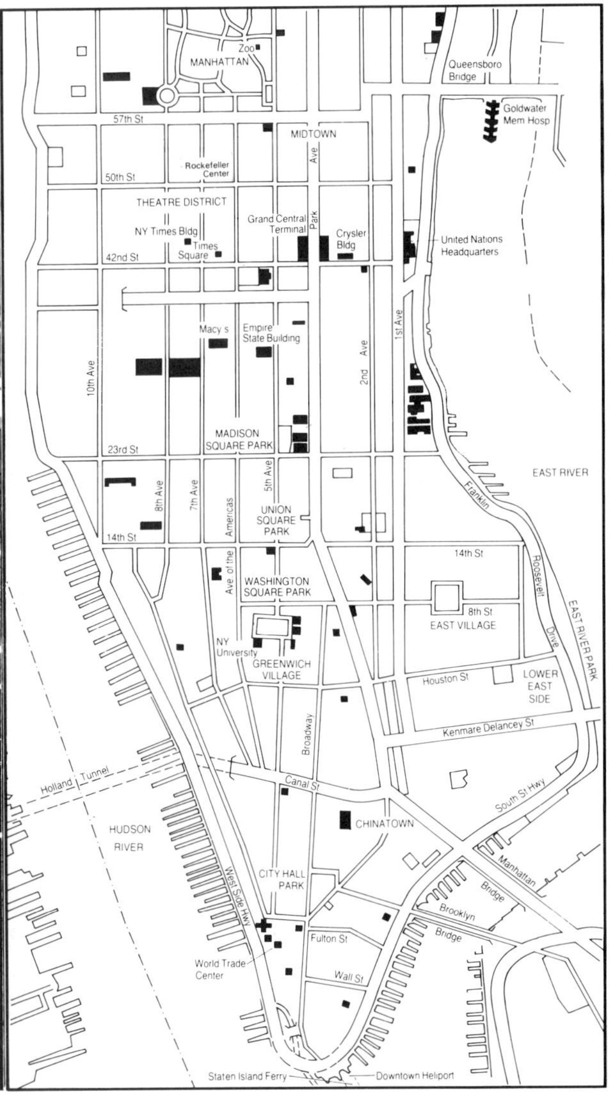

STEP THREE *James 'Jonah' Bartley*

There is a story in the Bible about a man called Jonah who was swallowed by a whale. Impossible? Well, it *could* have been true. An Englishman, James Bartley, has proved it.

On 25 August, 1891, a whaling ship, the *Star of the East*, was in the South Atlantic, when a look-out sighted a large whale. When they got close enough, a harpoon was fired and the whale was hit and wounded. A small boat was then lowered and half a dozen men rowed after the whale.

Suddenly, the whale turned and came straight towards them. Its huge mouth was wide open. With one bite, the small boat was crushed to splinters. The crew just had time to jump into the sea, but James Bartley was too slow. The whale's jaws closed, with Bartley between them. Then the whale sank below the surface.

The rest of the crew were later picked up by the *Star of the East*. They were all certain they had seen the last of James Bartley.

Later the same day the whale came to the surface – dead. It was tied to the side of their ship and the crew then spent the next two days cutting it up.

When they finally reached the whale's stomach, they were amazed to find James Bartley inside it – unconscious but still alive. Twelve hours later he was completely recovered. But for months afterwards his skin was purple from the acid in the whale's stomach.

Bartley later described how he felt live fish moving around him in the whale's stomach before he became unconscious.

For the rest of his life he was always called James 'Jonah' Bartley.

6. Interview Jonah Bartley

Complete the questions, and then answer them. Work in pairs. One of you is Jonah Bartley.

1 When ______ you swallowed by a whale?
2 What ______ the name of the ship you ______ on?
3 Where ______ it sailing?
4 ______ the whale killed immediately by the harpoon?
5 ______ you go after the wounded whale?
6 Why ______ *you* eaten and not the rest of the crew?
7 How ______ it feel inside the whale's stomach?
8 How long ______ you in there?
9 How long ______ you take to recover?

7. Make true sentences

<table>
<tr>
<td>A small boat
Bartley
The whale
A harpoon
The crew
The boat</td>
<td>was
were</td>
<td>called 'Jonah' for the rest of his life.
wounded.
lowered.
picked up later by the Star of the East.
tied to the side of the ship.
sighted by a look-out.
fired.
amazed to find Bartley inside the whale.
ordered to follow the whale.
crushed to splinters.
swallowed by the whale.</td>
</tr>
</table>

8. Complete the sentences

Use:

On 25 August	When
12 hours later	Then
For months afterwards	Later
Suddenly	For the rest

1 ______ a look-out saw a large whale.
2 ______ the whale turned and came towards the boat.
3 ______ it swallowed Bartley, while the rest of the crew dived overboard.
4 ______ the whale came to the surface – dead.
5 ______ they cut open the whale they found Bartley in its stomach.
6 ______ he was quite well again.
7 ______ Bartley's skin was purple.
8 ______ of his life, people always called him 'Jonah' Bartley.

9. Discussion

Why do you think Bartley survived?
Do you know any other true stories of amazing survival?

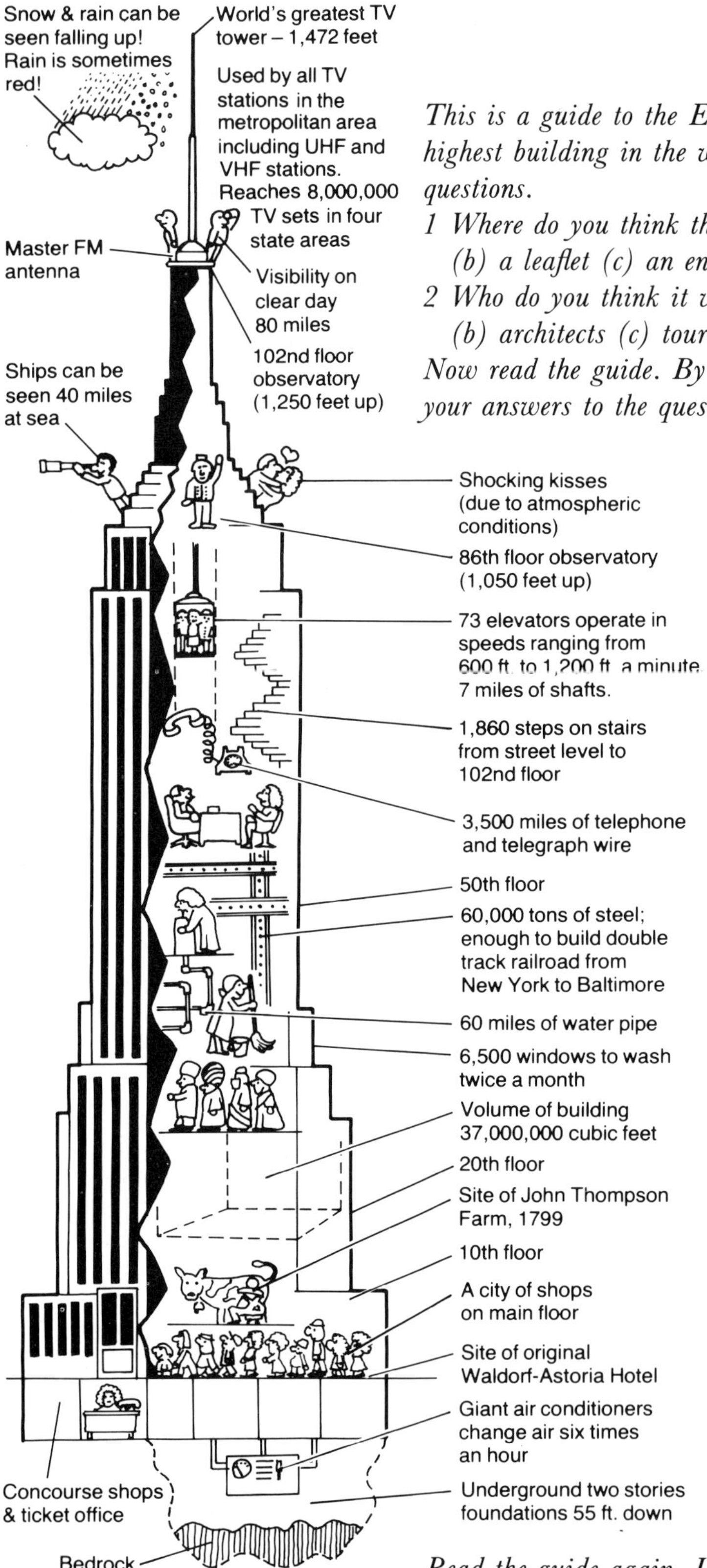

STEP FOUR ***City in the sky***

This is a guide to the Empire State Building in New York, the third highest building in the world. Before you read it, look at these questions.

1 Where do you think this guide comes from? (a) a newspaper (b) a leaflet (c) an encyclopaedia

2 Who do you think it was written for? (a) business people (b) architects (c) tourists

Now read the guide. By the end of it you should be able to discuss your answers to the questions above.

Facts about The Empire State Building

One of the world's eight wonders (The only one built in the 20th Century)

Thousands of post cards sold annually

Volume of building 37,000,000 cubic feet

Over a million and a half visitors from every state in US and nearly every foreign country visit "top of the Empire State" each year

2,000,000 square feet of rentable area (all outside space)

Read the guide again. If possible, work out the meaning of new words or, if you can't, look them up in a dictionary.

10. Reading comprehension

Match the questions with the correct answers.

Example: *How high is the 102nd floor? – 1,250 feet.*

How often is the air in the building changed?

When was John Thompson's farm built?

How high is the 102nd floor?

How often are the windows washed?

How many visitors are there a year?

How many steps do you have to climb to get up to the 102nd floor?

How high is the television tower?

How many elevators are there in the building?

How many windows are there in the building?

How much steel is there in the building?

Twice a month.

Six times an hour.

60,000 tons.

1,250 feet.

73.

6,500.

1,860.

1799.

1½ million.

1,472 feet.

11. Listening comprehension

Listen to the tape and write down what the guide is talking about.

12. Writing

Describe a famous building in your country. Include as many facts and statistics as you can.

13. Discussion

1 What would you like to visit if you had a holiday in the USA?
2 Do you think it is better for cities to grow 'upwards' or 'outwards'?

Grammar summary

I He She It	was	picked up.
You We They	were	

The statue	was	taken to pieces,	put into crates and	sent to America.

STEP ONE *The future of transport*

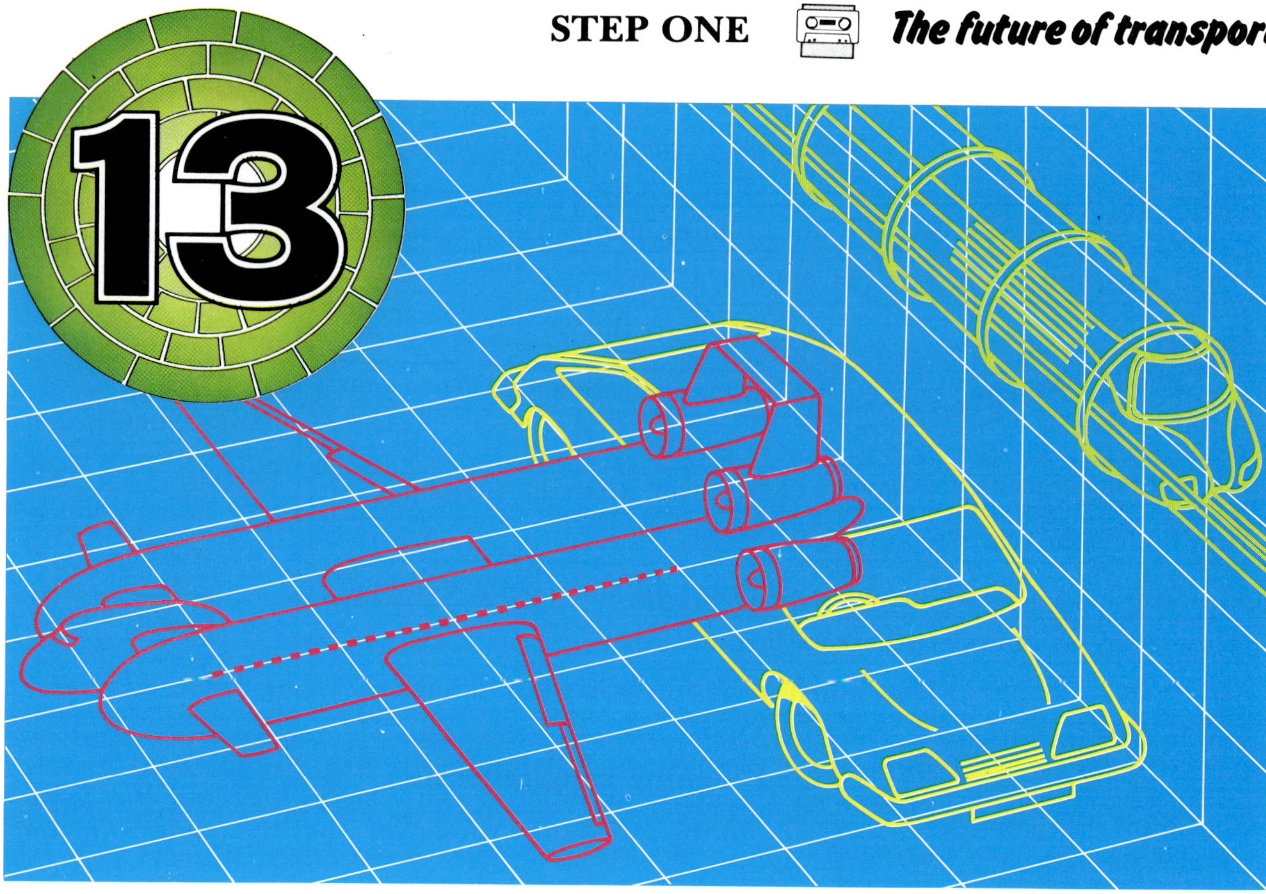

In the future trains may use 'magnetic levitation'. Electro-magnets in the train are attracted by magnets in the track in front, but repelled by other magnets in the track under the train. This means that the train will not actually touch the track but will 'float' over it.

In addition, the train will run in a vacuum tunnel. As a result there will be no friction of any kind, and trains like this will have a maximum speed of as much as 2,000 kph.

Cars in the future will probably be powered by electricity from completely new types of battery, one tenth the weight of batteries today. Because of this, and because they will be made of plastic and aluminium, cars will be extremely light. As a result, they will be very economical.

Computers will do almost everything for the driver. They will even tell him the best way to get to his destination by avoiding any traffic jams on the road ahead.

Most of the planes flying today were designed before the dramatic rise in fuel costs of the 70s. Planes in the future will definitely be far more economical because of new types of jet engine, new shapes and new materials. A twin-fuselage plane might fly by the end of the century.

As a result of these changes, the cost of flying will come down dramatically, and planes will probably be used even for short inter-city trips.

1. Make true sentences

Trains Cars Planes	in the future	might may		be very economical. run in a vacuum tunnel. have new types of jet engines. 'float' over a track. be made of plastic or aluminium. use magnetic levitation. be powered by electricity. have a maximum speed of 2,000 kph. be used for short inter-city trips. be extremely light. have twin fuselages.
		will	probably definitely	

2. Comparisons

Compare trains, cars and planes using these adjectives:

fast	slow	expensive	cheap
comfortable	dangerous	safe	

Examples: Planes are *faster than* trains.
Trains are *not as fast as* planes.

1 train/car
2 train/plane
3 car/train
4 car/plane
5 plane/train
6 plane/car

3. Ask a friend

Ask how often he/she travels by train/car.
if he/she has ever flown in a plane. (Where did he/she fly to?)
what the maximum speed he/she has travelled at is.
if he/she has got anything made of plastic on him/her.
what form of transport he/she usually uses to go to another city.

4. Finish the sentences

Finish these sentences in any way you like.

By the end of the century I	might may		. . .
	will	probably definitely	

STEP TWO Football failures

To be a professional footballer must be one of the most difficult jobs to get and, even more, to keep. Three quarters of the boys who become apprentices at the age of sixteen will be 'finished' by the time they're twenty-one.

It's no use telling them that they only have a fifty-fifty chance of being offered a job as a full-time professional when they are eighteen – because of course *they* are going to be the lucky ones. And while they are apprentices, they spend most of their time dreaming about playing for the first team.

Rob Newman grew up in Newcastle and left school as soon as he possibly could – it wasn't worth staying on to take any exams. He was going to be a professional footballer with a top London team.

'A professional contract on my sixteenth birthday! I couldn't believe it. I was homesick at first, living away from home, down in London. I remember I used to go to sleep at night thinking, right, next step's the reserves. Then, when I'm about eighteen, the first team. In fact, I improved a lot as a player. But then, suddenly, when I was eighteen, the manager called me in one day and told me, "Sorry, you're not good enough." "You're not serious," I said. But he was. I couldn't believe it! I cried like a baby, I remember. But it was no good arguing. I just had to pack my bags and come back here to Newcastle, where three out of every four teenagers are unemployed. So of course I'm on the dole.'

'But I can't stand doing nothing so I keep fit by running every day and by playing for a local amateur team. And I still hope a scout from one of the big clubs will come along and notice me.'

'But I can't help thinking I've had my chance and I won't get another. I'm a failure – at nineteen!'

5. Interview Rob Newman

Fill in the missing question words first, then ask and answer in pairs.

1 ______ did you grow up?
2 ______ did you leave school?
3 ______ didn't you stay on at school?
4 ______ did you go when you were sixteen?
5 ______ did you feel, living away from home?
6 ______ happened when you were eighteen?
7 ______ did you feel?
8 ______ did you go?
9 ______ do you do every day now?
10 ______ are you hoping?

6. Finish the sentences

Write about yourself.

1 I can't help . . .
2 It's not worth . . .
3 I can't stand . . .
4 It's no use . . .

7. Dialogues

Write three-line dialogues like this:

– It's not worth *leaving school at the age of sixteen.*
– Why not?
– Because *there are no jobs for sixteen-year-olds with no exams.*

Replace the words in italics with your own ideas. Act out the dialogues in pairs.

8. You're not good enough

Complete the dialogue.

Manager	Rob Newman
Tell Rob to come in.	Ask why the manager wants to see you.
Tell Rob you've got bad news for him.	Ask what it is.
Tell him he won't get a new contract.	Express disbelief.
Sympathise with Rob.	Ask why you won't get a new contract.
Explain.	Break down.

9. You're not serious!

Work in pairs. One student says something very surprising and the other reacts by saying: You're not serious! or I can't believe it!

Example: – *It's the end of the lesson.*
– *You're not serious! It's only twenty past ten.*

STEP THREE *Half-way home*

Mr Enrico Viscardi was an Italian immigrant living in the Italian quarter of San Francisco. Although he had been in the United States for over five years, he'd learnt very little English.

He worked hard and eventually he'd saved up enough money to return to his native Naples for a holiday.

He took off from San Francisco Airport, and after he'd had a large in-flight dinner and a few drinks he fell asleep.

When he woke up he was relieved to find the plane had just landed. He was pleased that the long transatlantic flight was over, but he was disappointed that his nephews hadn't come to meet him at Rome Airport. He decided to go and wait for them at their flat.

He was surprised to see how much Rome had changed. He was also amazed at the number of American tourists. They were everywhere!

After he'd got off the bus, he asked a policeman the way. The policeman, he was relieved to find, also came from Naples. But, to his surprise, the next person he asked for help did not understand him. Mr Viscardi knew he had a Naples accent, but he hadn't realised it was so strong!

He then showed the address of his nephews' flat to a policeman.

'But this address is in Rome,' said the policeman, in English. 'And we're in the middle of New York!'

Mr Viscardi's plane had, in fact, landed in New York to refuel. By the time the flight for Rome was called, Mr Viscardi had already left the airport.

The police decided to rush him to the airport to catch the next flight to Rome. Mr Viscardi, however, was still convinced he was already there.

'You see,' he said, 'I know I'm in Rome because this is how they always drive in Italy!'

10. Make sentences

Make full sentences with one verb in the past perfect, the other in the past simple.

Example: live in San Francisco/buy a house
After he *had lived* in San Francisco for three years, he *bought* a house.

1 live in the USA/learn very little English
2 save up/go back to Naples
3 have a large dinner/go to sleep
4 wake up/land
5 leave the airport/wait for half an hour
6 get off the bus/ask a policeman
7 find out the time of the next flight to Rome/rush him to the airport

11. Write sentences

Example: *Enrico Viscardi was relieved when he found that the plane had landed.*

Enrico Viscardi was	pleased disappointed relieved surprised amazed	when	. . .

12. Write about yourself

I'm	pleased disappointed relieved surprised amazed	when	. . .

13. A postcard

Imagine you are Enrico Viscardi. Write a postcard to a friend back in San Francisco explaining what happened to you in New York.

14. Listen for the information

1 Flight number: ______
2 Gate number: ______
3 Seat number: ______
4 Height: ______
5 Speed: ______
6 Time of arrival in Rome: ______
7 Temperature: ______

STEP FOUR ***Seeing the sights***

This is a page from a tourist guide to London. Before you read it, look at these questions.

1 What is Oxford Street famous for?

2 Who was the architect of St. Paul's Cathedral?

3 What can you see in the middle of Trafalgar Square?

Now read the extract from the tourist guide. At the end of it you should know the answers to the three questions above.

St. Paul's Cathedral

Work on Sir Christopher Wren's greatest church was first begun in 1675, nine years after the original St. Paul's was destroyed in the Great Fire of London. Since the Second World War, bomb-damaged stained glass has been replaced with clear glass, as originally planned by Wren. This has made the interior of the cathedral look even larger. Visitors can climb up to the Whispering Gallery. There you can hear a whisper from the other side of the dome, 30 metres away. Christopher Wren, Lord Nelson and the Duke of Wellington are buried in St. Paul's.

Oxford Street

Oxford Street is over 1½ kilometres long and the most popular shopping street in London. It is particularly famous for its many large department stores. At the western end is Marble Arch, which was designed by John Nash in 1828. The arch was originally meant to be the entrance to Buckingham Palace, the royal residence. Speakers' Corner, just inside Hyde Park, is an open space where anyone may speak about anything. It is liveliest on Sundays, when large crowds gather to listen to the many speakers on every possible subject – and to the people who interrupt and argue with them.

Trafalgar Square

This is London's most famous square, designed to commemorate Lord Nelson's great naval victory against the French in 1805. In the middle is Nelson's Column. The 5-metre statue of the Admiral is at the top, 55 metres above the ground. At the bottom of the column there are four bronze lions, one for each of Lord Nelson's greatest naval victories. Thousands of tourists buy special food for the pigeons, and then have their photographs taken with pigeons sitting on their hands, shoulders or heads. On the north side of the square is the National Gallery, which has one of the world's finest collections of paintings.

Read the text again carefully. If possible, work out the meaning of new words or, if you can't, look them up in a dictionary.

15. Reading comprehension

Choose the correct alternative.

1 The Great Fire of London was in (a) 1666.
(b) 1675.
(c) 1684.

2 Wren (a) wanted stained glass in St. Paul's.
(b) built the original
(c) is buried in

3 Speakers' Corner is (a) only open on Sundays.
(b) in Oxford Street.
(c) most popular on Sundays.

4 The pigeons (a) buy food in Trafalgar Square.
(b) have their photographs taken.
(c) stand on their heads.

16. Listening comprehension

Listen to the tape and write down where in London the people are, using the information in the text.

17. Writing

Write short paragraphs describing a famous street or monument in your country.

18. Discussion

1 If a foreign visitor in your area had only one day to spend, what would you recommend him/her to visit?
2 'Travel broadens the mind.' Do you think this is true?

Grammar summary

The cost of flying	will may might	(not)	go down.

After As soon as When	he had eaten,	he fell asleep.

I	can't	help stand	forgetting things.

It's	not worth no use	waiting.

I keep fit	by	running.
They dream	about	playing.

14

STEP ONE

The A to Z of Britain and the USA

A is for **air conditioning**. They have it in cars, offices and houses all over the USA. In Britain it's not necessary – it's rarely hot enough!

B is for **breakfast**, which Americans often have in fast food places. In Britain, some people say that to eat well you should have three traditional British breakfasts a day!

C is for **coffee**, which in the USA is good and, after the first cup, usually free. In Britain, it's often so terrible you wouldn't drink it even if it *was* free!

D is for **doctors**, who in the USA are so expensive you can't afford to be ill. In Britain they charge you nothing, even if you're a foreigner!

E is for **electricity**. In the USA it's not so easy to electrocute yourself – the voltage is only 110. In Britain it's 240 volts.

F is for **football**. In American football the ball is egg-shaped and you throw it or run with it. They call 'real' football 'soccer'!

G is for **gum**, which in the USA is so popular many people chew it all the time!

H is for **hurricanes**, which are quite frequent in the south of the USA. In Britain there's nothing as exciting as a hurricane. It just rains.

I is for **insects**, which in the USA can sting, bite and poison you. In Britain they're not so dangerous. They just annoy you.

J is for **jogging**, which became a craze in the USA before it spread to other countries. It's now popular in Britain, too!

K is for **kettles**, which in Britain are almost always electric. In the USA they are not nearly so common – you have to boil water in a pan.

L is for **language**. British English is not 'better' or 'more correct' than American English. The two are just different dialects.

M is for **motels**. Americans almost always stay in motels (motor hotels). British people stay in a hotel or a 'bed and breakfast'.

N is for **newspapers**. In the USA there aren't really any national newspapers – the country is too big. In Britain there are eight national newspapers.

O is for **oil**. Most of the oil in the USA is under the ground. British oil has to be obtained from under the sea.

P is for **police**. In the USA they carry guns and are not always friendly. In Britain they *don't* carry guns and are, usually, quite friendly.

Q is for **queen**. They don't have or need a king or queen in the USA. In Britain most people still believe they need a monarch.

R is for **radio**, which in Britain usually means the BBC. In the USA, most radio stations are local and much smaller, and play pop music more or less non-stop.

S is for **speed limit**. On American roads you mustn't drive at more than 90 kph. The top speed limit on British roads is 110 kph.

T is for **time zones**. The USA is so wide that it has to have four time zones – or six, if you include Alaska!

U is for **universities**. In Britain students don't need to pay to go to university. In the USA parents, or students themselves, have to pay.

V is for **violence**, which is more common in the USA than in Britain. But only a few parts of the big American cities are actually unsafe.

W is for **weather**. In the USA it varies enormously. In Britain it's never very hot, or very cold, but often quite wet – so an umbrella is usually a good idea!

X is for **Xerox**, which in American English means 'to photocopy'.

Y is for **Yanks** or **Yankees**, which in British English is an unfriendly term for Americans. Americans themselves only use it to mean people from the north-east of the USA.

Z is for **zip code**, which is part of every US address. In Britain it's called the postal code, but you don't *have* to use it!

STEP TWO

1. Write true sentences

Write sentences like this, using the information in the text.

In the USA you *mustn't* drive at more than 90 kph. In Britain you *mustn't* drive at more than 110 kph.
In Britain you *don't have to* pay to see a doctor. In the USA you *have to*.
The USA *needs* four time zones. Britain only *needs* one.

2. Write about your country

In this country we	have to don't have to mustn't	. . .

Think of two examples for each.

3. Comparisons

Compare the following things in your country with the same things in Britain *or* the USA, in any way you like.

breakfasts	police
doctors	radio
insects	speed limits
language	universities
newspapers	violence
oil	weather

4. Discussion

Is your country more like Britain or the USA?

5. Where would you go?

If you could choose between visiting the USA or visiting Britain, which would you choose? Write five reasons.

Example: I'd prefer to visit the USA because . . .

6. Comparisons

Compare your country and Britain *or* the USA, using this table:

There	isn't	so much	. . .	in	Britain.
	aren't	so many			the USA.

First make a statement about your country.

Example: *There's a lot of coffee in Brazil.*

Then compare this statement with Britain or the USA.

Example: *There isn't so much in the USA.*

7. Write about your country

Think of your own sentences like this:

The	. . .	in this country	is are	so	beautiful terrible good expensive cheap . . .	. . .

Example: *The doctors in this country are so expensive you can't afford to be ill.*

8. Where are they?

Listen to the tape and decide if the speakers are in Britain or the USA.

From grass to concrete

STEP THREE

Moles 3 Mr Ferris 0

A businessman, Mr Edward Ferris (42), has had to stop trying to get rid of the moles under his lawn. But only after he had accidentally destroyed his new £20,000 Jaguar and caused serious damage to his house near Bourne in Lincolnshire.

Things went badly wrong when Mr Ferris decided that he had to poison the moles which had been ruining his front lawn for over a year.

'I had to park my car in the middle of the lawn after midnight, when the moles are usually most active,' explained Mr Ferris. 'I left the car lights on so I could see what I was doing. Unfortunately, it was a new car and I wasn't used to its automatic gearbox so I put it into reverse by mistake. The car shot backwards into the front wall of my house. Part of the wall fell down on top of my car. The petrol tank was punctured – it was full because I had to go on a trip to France the next day – and an electric fire in the front room of my house set fire to the petrol. The car then caught fire, and so did the house. With the telephone wires burnt through, I couldn't phone the fire brigade so I had to wake up a neighbour and use his phone. But it was too late.'

Today Mr Ferris is left with no car, only half a house – and a lawn with over twenty new molehills on it.

'I have to admit it – the moles have won. I know when I'm beaten!' said a defeated Mr Ferris. 'I'll just have to order ten tons of concrete to pour over what is left of my lawn!'

9. Questions and answers

First work out the eight questions, then ask and answer in pairs.

Why did Mr Ferris	want leave wake up fill order park put phone	it into reverse by mistake? the fire brigade? his car on the lawn? ten tons of concrete? to get rid of the moles? his car with petrol? the car lights on? a neighbour?

10. What will he have to do?

Think of what Mr Ferris will have to do in the following situations. Then act out the two-line dialogues in pairs.

Example: – There are moles underneath my lawn.
– *You'll have to poison them.*

1 I'm going on a trip to France tomorrow.
2 My house is on fire.
3 The telephone wires are burnt down.
4 My neighbour is asleep.
5 My car is destroyed.
6 The front wall of my house has fallen down.
7 There are still moles under the lawn.

11. I have to get up at 7 o'clock

Complete the following sentences. Use different ideas for each sentence.

Every day I have to . . .
Yesterday I had to . . .
Recently I have had to . . .
Tomorrow I will have to . . .

Now ask each other questions.

Example: *What do you have to do every day?*

12. Complete the sentences

Put the right form of the verb 'have to' in the following sentences.

Example: He *had to* phone the fire brigade.

1 Mr Ferris . . . go to France quite often.
2 He . . . not . . . go by car.
3 Last night he . . . wake up a neighbour in the middle of the night.
4 He . . . buy a new car next week.
5 He . . . have a car for business.
6 Builders . . . repair his house next month.

Now write sentences about yourself using 'have to', 'had to', and 'will have to'.

13. A dialogue

Complete this dialogue between Mr Ferris and his neighbour.

Mr Ferris: ______ sorry ______ disturb ______ . ______ I use ______ phone?
Neighbour: ______ for?
Mr Ferris: I ______ to ______ the fire brigade.
Neighbour: ______the problem?
Mr Ferris: ______ house ______ car ______ on fire.
Neighbour: How ______ it happen?
Mr Ferris: ______ long story. ______ can't ______ you now!

Now practise the dialogue in pairs.

STEP FOUR *Hurricane!*

This series of warnings and tips is printed on shopping bags given to customers by a large supermarket in Miami, Florida, USA. Before you read the text, look at these questions.

1 What sort of things should you do before *there is a hurricane warning?*

2 What sort of things should you do after *there is a hurricane warning?*

3 What sort of things should you do when a hurricane arrives?

Now read the text. By the end of it you should know the answers to the questions above. Answer them orally.

Here are some tips in the event a hurricane approaches.

Be prepared

Hurricanes mean damage from wind and water. They also can mean a day or two of isolation – you and your family must be able to go it alone. Make sure you have what you need – materials for protecting windows and glass doors, non-perishable food items, containers for drinking water, flashlights, matches, candles, portable radio or television and batteries. These items get in short supply of an approaching hurricane – don't wait until the last minute to stock up.

When your area receives a hurricane warning

Leave low lying areas.
Moor your boat securely or evacuate it.
Protect your windows with boards, shutters or tape.
Secure outdoor objects or bring them indoors.
Fuel your car.
Save several days' water supply.
Stay at home if it is sturdy and on high ground.
Leave mobile homes for more substantial shelter.
Stay indoors during the hurricane.
Listen for Weather Service hurricane bulletins.

YOU WILL NOT BE ASKED TO LEAVE YOUR HOME UNLESS YOUR LIFE IS SERIOUSLY THREATENED. WHEN YOU RECEIVE WORD TO LEAVE, GO!

When a hurricane strikes

Stay out of heavily damaged or flooded areas.
Avoid loose or dangling wires.
Prevent fires. Low water pressure makes them hard to fight.
Check refrigerated food for spoilage if power has been off during the storm.
Cooperate with emergency forces and officials.
If your area is threatened by hurricane-spawned tornadoes, take shelter inside, in small interior areas like hallways, closets and bathrooms.

Weather Words

Hurricane Watch: Hurricane may threaten within 24 hours.

Hurricane Warning: Hurricane expected to strike within 24 hours.

Tropical Depression: A cyclone with winds of less than 39 MPH or 34 KNOTS.

Tropical Storm: A cyclone with winds from 39 to 73 MPH or 34 to 63 KNOTS.

Hurricane: A violent cyclone with winds of greater than 74 MPH or 64 KNOTS.

June through November is Florida's Hurricane Season.

Read the text again carefully. If possible, work out the meaning of new words or, if you can't, look them up in a dictionary.

14. Reading comprehension

Which of these things *should* you do and which should you *not* do after a hurricane warning?

1 Go out and buy a portable radio.
2 Fill your car up with petrol.
3 Buy plenty of perishable food.
4 Make sure the glass in your windows is protected.
5 Bring things like garden chairs into the house.
6 If you live on a boat, stay on it.
7 Fill your bath and basins with water.
8 Stay in your home, however bad the hurricane is.

15. Listening comprehension

Listen to the hurricane warning on the tape and then answer these questions.

1 Which television channel is the hurricane warning on?
2 What time was this Weather Word broadcast?
3 What is the name of the hurricane?
4 Where is it now?
5 How fast is it moving?
6 In which direction is it moving?
7 When will it reach Miami?
8 How fast are the winds expected to be?

16. Writing

Write a dialogue between two people who live near Miami. They have just heard a hurricane warning. Write the conversation as they check that they are prepared. Use phrases like:

Are you sure we have . . .?
Did you remember to . . .?
I think we should . . .
Why don't we . . .?
Let's . . .

17. Discussion

1 If you knew that a hurricane was going to destroy your home and you had only five minutes to save the things you value most, which things would you save?
2 'People who choose to live in a hurricane or earthquake zone have no right to expect help from the government if their homes are destroyed.' Do you agree?

Grammar summary

American students	have to must	pay to go to university.

They're not	so	popular. dangerous. expensive.

<table>
<tr><td rowspan="3">I
You
He
She
We
They</td><td colspan="2">had</td><td rowspan="3">to</td><td rowspan="3">buy a new car.</td></tr>
<tr><td>(didn't)</td><td rowspan="2">have</td></tr>
<tr><td>will
(won't)</td></tr>
</table>

The USA is	so	wide	(that)	it has to have four time zones.

15

STEP ONE ***Crying in the night (1)***

My friend Sebastian didn't really want to live in the country, miles away from anywhere. He was quite happy in his flat in London. But when his father died and left the family house to Sebastian, he decided he couldn't sell it. After all, it had been in his family for generations.

One weekend he invited me down to have a look at it. I arrived late on a Friday evening. It was a large eighteenth-century house surrounded by its own park and woodland.

Sebastian had heard my car and was waiting at the front door to welcome me. It was too late to look over the house, so we had dinner and talked until midnight. Then Sebastian showed me up to my room. It was small but comfortable, and I soon fell asleep.

It was at 2.45 that I suddenly woke up. I knew that was the time because I happened to look at my watch. Normally, I sleep deeply until my alarm clock wakes me in the morning. So why was I wide awake now, in the middle of the night?

Then I heard it – the sound of a baby crying. It sounded strangely close, but I couldn't tell exactly where it was coming from. It went on for about a minute. Then it suddenly rose to a scream – and stopped, with a kind of choking sound.

I couldn't understand it. The nearest house was over three kilometres away, in the village. Sebastian had said nothing about other visitors in the house, and certainly not a baby.

I slept badly after that. I had one nightmare after another. But I heard no more crying.

1. Finish the sentences

1 Sebastian didn't want to live in the country because . . .
2 He decided he couldn't sell the house because . . .
3 Sebastian was waiting at the front door because . . .
4 They didn't look over the house because . . .
5 Charles woke up in the middle of the night because . . .
6 He knew it was 2.45 because . . .
7 It was unusual for Charles to wake up at this time because . . .
8 He couldn't understand the noise because . . .
9 He was sure there was no baby in the house because . . .
10 Charles slept badly for the rest of the night because . . .

2. What are the missing question words?

Fill in the missing words in the questions, then ask and answer in pairs.

1 ______ didn't Sebastian want to live in the country?
2 ______ left the house to Sebastian?
3 ______ old was it?
4 ______ did Charles arrive at the house?
5 ______ was the bedroom like?
6 ______ time did he wake up?
7 ______ did he know?
8 ______ did the noise end?
9 ______ was the nearest house?
10 ______ did he sleep after that?

3. A letter

Write a letter in which Sebastian explains why he has moved out of London, describes his house in the country and invites Charles to stay for the weekend.

4. Discussion

How do you think the story continues? Discuss your ideas in groups.

STEP TWO *Crying in the night (2)*

Over breakfast the next morning I told Sebastian what had happened. He looked more guilty than surprised.

'I'm sorry, Charles,' he said. 'I shouldn't have let you sleep in that room.'

'What do you mean? What's wrong with the room?'

'There's nothing *wrong* with it, exactly – it's just that . . . No.'

'Well, go on! You've started now.'

'Well, my grandfather always used to tell us a story about something which happened in this house at the end of the last century, when *his* father was a child.'

Sebastian paused while he poured himself another cup of tea.

'Well, come on, then!' I said.

[illegible]stian sipped his tea slowly and then [illegible]n.

'It was a warm summer's night, and they left the bedroom windows open. A thief climbed in through one of them, into the bedroom of the youngest child of the family, who was a baby girl, only six months old. The thief made too much noise climbing in, so he woke the baby. When she started to cry, he was afraid he'd be discovered, so he panicked and put a pillow over the baby's face to try and smother the noise.'

'But, in his panic, he pressed too hard and for too long, and the baby suffocated. The thief then escaped out of the window. But he was caught the next day and confessed everything. He was later hanged for the murder of the baby.'

'But the most interesting part of the story is that the murder was committed in *your* room between half past two and three in the morning. The baby you heard crying last night died exactly a hundred years ago.'

5. Tell the story

Put the sentences in the right order.

They had breakfast.
The crying rose to a scream.
Charles went to bed.
Sebastian told him about the murder.
Charles heard a baby crying.
They had dinner.
Charles told Sebastian what had happened during the night.

6. Discussion

What do you think happened? Discuss whether the following statements are true or false.

1 Charles heard a baby crying.
2 He only dreamed he heard a baby crying.
3 The ghost of the baby was still in the room.
4 Sebastian played a joke on Charles.

7. Ask each other

Do you believe: you can hear ghosts?
you can see ghosts?
you can talk to ghosts?
you can communicate in any way with people who are dead?
some buildings are haunted?

Find out what the majority of your class thinks.

8. A dialogue

Write the conversation between Charles and a friend when he gets back to London and tells his friend what happened.

Act out the dialogue in pairs.

STEP THREE

9. Which is right?

1 Sebastian didn't want / wanted not / didn't wanted to leave his flat in London.

2 Sebastian decided he didn't can / couldn't / can't sell the house.

3 It had been / have been / was been in his family for generations.

4 Charles was invited down for to have / for having / to have a look at the house.

5 Normally his alarm clock wake / does wake / woke him up in the morning.

6 He heard the sound of a baby cry. / crying. / to cry.

7 The nearest / The most near / Nearest house was over 3 kilometres away.

8 Sebastian had not said nothing / had said nothing / had not said something about visitors in the house.

9 'I shouldn't have let you to sleep / sleeping / sleep in that room.'

10 His grandfather always use to / used to / did use to tell a story about the house.

11 The thief murdered the youngest child of the family, that / which / who was a baby girl.

12 He was caught / were caught / did he caught the next day.

13 The most interesting / The most interested / The most interestingest part of the story was the time the murder was committed.

14 The baby died before a hundred years. / a hundred years ago. / since a hundred years.

10. The murder

Listen to the tape and fill in the missing words below.

The __(1)__ was caught by the police only a short __(2)__ away. When he was __(3)__, he __(4)__ that he was __(5)__ of murdering the baby but said he had not __(6)__ to. He was only a common __(7)__ who had __(8)__ in through a bedroom window. He had __(9)__ when the baby started __(10)__ and had put a __(11)__ over her face but he had not meant to __(12)__ her.

11. A report

Complete this newspaper report.

THE TIMES

FRIDAY, 13 AUGUST, 1886.

HORRIBLE MURDER

MAN HELD

Devon police announced last night that a man has been arrested in connection with the murder of Miss Alexandra Flyte, daughter of Sir Henry Flyte. The man is believed to have given a full confession.

The murder took place at Hardacre Hall, home of the Flyt- family

STEP FOUR *Savages*

These are two short passages from the novel Lord of the Flies *by the English writer, William Golding. Before you read them, look at these questions.*
1 Where are the boys and why are they there?
2 What do Ralph and Jack argue about?
3 Why is the fire so important?
Now read the text. By the end of it, you should know the answers to the three questions above. Answer them orally.

(After the outbreak of a World War, a plane crash-lands on a tropical island. On board are a party of schoolboys. No adults survive the crash. Ralph, one of the older boys, becomes the leader. They discuss how to organise things, keep a fire going in case someone on a passing ship should see it, and hunt for food. Jack is jealous of Ralph, and he becomes the leader of a 'tribe' of boys who are only interested in hunting. Finally, Ralph and Jack meet to decide things. Note: 'specs' are glasses.)

Jack shouted, 'You go away, Ralph. You keep to your end. This is my end and my tribe. You leave me alone.'

'You pinched Piggy's specs,' said Ralph, breathlessly. 'You've got to give them back.'

'Got to? Who says?'

'I say! You voted for me for Chief. You played a dirty trick – we'd have given you fire if you'd asked for it – '

The blood was flowing in his cheeks.

'You could have had a fire whenever you wanted. But you didn't. You came sneaking up like a thief and stole Piggy's glasses!'

'Say that again!'

'Thief! Thief!'

Jack made a rush and stabbed at Ralph's chest with his spear . . .

(The two boys begin fighting. Suddenly Piggy cries out, 'Ralph – remember what we came for. The fire. My specs!' The fight stops, and Ralph starts talking to Jack and his tribe.)

'Listen. We've come to say this. First you've got to give back Piggy's specs. If he hasn't got them he can't see. You aren't playing the game –'

The tribe of painted savages giggled and Ralph's mind faltered. He pushed his hair up and gazed at the green and black mask before him, trying to remember what Jack looked like.

Piggy whispered, 'And the fire.'

'Oh yes. Then about the fire. I say this again. I've been saying it ever since we came.'

He held out his spear and pointed at the savages.

'Your only hope is keeping a signal fire going as long as there's light to see. Then maybe a ship'll notice the smoke and come and rescue us and take us home. But without that smoke we've got to wait till some ship comes by accident. We might wait for years, till we're old –'

Now read the text again carefully. If possible, work out the meaning of new words or, if you can't, look them up in a dictionary.

12. Reading comprehension

Choose the best alternatives, according to the text.

1 The boys are on the island because
(a) their plane crash-landed there.
(b) some adults left them there.
(c) there's going to be a World War.

2 Ralph (a) is jealous of Jack.
(b) wants Jack to give Piggy back his glasses.
(c) is leader of the hunters.

3 Jack (a) wants Ralph to leave him and his tribe alone.
(b) wants to give Piggy's glasses back.
(c) is attacked by Ralph.

4 Ralph (a) has painted himself green and black.
(b) wants to play a game.
(c) has almost forgotten what Jack looks like.

5 A fire (a) may rescue them.
(b) may be seen from a ship.
(c) may be started by accident.

13. Listening comprehension

Listen to the tape and decide who you think might say the sentences – Ralph, Jack or Piggy.

14. Writing

Imagine a situation in which the leaders of two groups or gangs meet and argue. Describe the reason why they are arguing and then write a short dialogue.

15. Discussion

1 If you were in the same situation as the boys on the island, how do you think *you* would react?
2 'Civilisation is only skin deep.' Do you think this is true?

Vocabulary

This list contains the new words introduced in each unit. They are listed in the order in which they appear in the text. (Words introduced in the authentic reading material in Step Four are not included.)

Unit one

corner
unlock (v)
drums
cheerful
care
reckon (v)
computer
memory
revise (v)
not – either
there's no point
mystery
fisherman
repair (v)
sailing ship
run aground (v)
warning
direction
row (v)
deck
reply
on board
sailor
below
stove
plate
violence
crew
desert (v)
log

Unit two

wish (v)
keep on at (v)
well-worn
phrase
teenage
recently
include (v)
questionnaire
reader
exam
music
mirror
contact
rest
shed
shortwave
knob
radio set
high-pitched
repeat (v)
grab (v)
transmitter
light year
planet
explore (v)
investigate (v)
weird
position
precisely
bitterly
disappointed
crunching
saucer-shaped
result
burst out (v)
keep something to yourself (v)
yell (v)
trust
out of sight
step
notice board
obviously
control yourself (v)
fail (v)
prepare yourself (v)
in-between
furiously
slouch (v)
defeated
joy

Unit three

graph
weight
rapidly
catch up (v)
shrink (v)
however
increase (v)
adolescence
particularly
lower
shape
jaw
stick out (v)
chin
pointed
slightly
accent
date (v) (US)
cute (US)
movie (US)
downtown (US)
vacation
fall (US)
gas (US)
railroad (US)
autumn
apartment
elevator (US)
sidewalk (US)
crosswalk (US)
pharmacy
pavement
pedestrian crossing
chemist's
cookie (US)
candy (US)
biscuit
sweet
get somebody down (v)
debate (v)
persuade (v)
debate
give up (v)
necessity
go flat (v)
cloud
eventually
get round to (v)
practically
ruin (v)

Unit four

for sale
unit
cupboard
agent
out of the question
disturb (v)
bee
communicate (v)
nectar
hive
step
rhythm
alligator
rattlesnake
whoever
nostril
cell
heat
mate (v)
tap (v)
sensitive
skin

Unit five

on business
might (v)
lift (v)
collect (v)
anger
pain
get on somebody's nerves (v)
behave (v)
keep out of somebody's way (v)
ought to (v)
reasonable
act (v)
research
anchor (v)
anchor
keep on (v)
ugly
biologist
reference
completely
species
unique
line
depth
harmless
sieve
soup
victim
shrimp